TEACHER EDUCATORS

IN THE TWENTY-FIRST CENTURY

Identity, knowledge and research

Critical Guides for
Teacher Educators

You might also like the following books in this series from Critical Publishing.

Ability Grouping in Primary Schools: Case Studies and Critical Debates
Rachel Marks
978-1-910391-24-2

Beginning Teachers' Learning: Making Experience Count
Katharine Burn, Hazel Hagger and Trevor Mutton
978-1-910391-17-4

Coteaching in Teacher Education: Innovative Pedagogy for Excellence
Colette Murphy
978-1-910391-82-2

Developing Creative and Critical Educational Practitioners
Victoria Door
978-1-909682-37-5

Developing Outstanding Practice in School-based Teacher Education
Edited by Kim Jones and Elizabeth White
978-1-909682-41-2

Evidence-based Teaching in Primary Education
Edited by Val Poultney
978-1-911196-46-3

How Do Expert Primary Classteachers Really Work? A Critical Guide for Teachers, Headteachers and Teacher Educators
Tony Eaude
978-1-909330-01-6

Teacher Status and Professional Learning: The Place Model
Linda Clarke
978-1-910391-46-4

Theories of Professional Learning
Carey Philpott
978-1-909682-33-7

Tackling Social Disadvantage through Teacher Education
Ian Thompson
978-1-912096-61-9

Our titles are also available in a range of electronic formats. To order please go to our website www.criticalpublishing.com or contact our distributor NBN International by telephoning 01752 202301 or emailing orders@nbninternational.com.

TEACHER EDUCATORS

IN THE TWENTY-FIRST CENTURY

Identity, knowledge and research

Series Editor: Ian Menter

Critical Guides for
Teacher Educators

Gerry **Czerniawski**

First published in 2018 by Critical Publishing Ltd

The author has made every effort to ensure the accuracy of information contained in this publication, but assumes no responsibility for any errors, inaccuracies, inconsistencies and omissions. Likewise every effort has been made to contact copyright holders. If any copyright material has been reproduced unwittingly and without permission the Publisher will gladly receive information enabling them to rectify any error or omission in subsequent editions.

British Library Cataloguing in Publication Data
A CIP record for this book is available from the British Library

ISBN: 9781912096534

This book is also available in the following e-book formats:
MOBI: 9781912096527
EPUB: 9781912096510
Adobe e-book reader: 9781912096503

The right of Gerry Czerniawski to be identified as the Author of this work has been asserted by him in accordance with the Copyright, Design and Patents Act 1988.

Cover and text design by Greensplash Limited
Project Management by Out of House Publishing
Typeset by Out of House Publishing
Printed and bound in Great Britain by 4edge, Essex

Critical Publishing
3 Connaught Road
St Albans
AL3 5RX

www.criticalpublishing.com

Paper from responsible sources

This book is dedicated to Kieran, Greg and Seamus Walsh, Huali Piao and Rian, Jes and Effie, 'Uncle Bob' and my wife, Jenny Barksfield. This wonderful disparate group of people constitute my very own reconstituted family – a family I love, respect and who constantly thrill and refill me with awe.

CONTENTS

ACKNOWLEDGEMENTS

I owe a huge debt of gratitude to Ian Menter who has, throughout my career, been an inspirational and generous educator and colleague. My thanks to both Ian Menter and Julia Morris at Critical Publishing and to Clare Owen at Out of House Publishing for their brilliant feedback and editorial support through each and every stage of the writing process. My colleagues at the International Forum for Teacher Educator Development (InFo-TED) continue to inspire so many aspects of my work and I hope I have done justice to them and the forum. The same is true for my colleagues at the University of East London and to its students who continue to thrill, amaze and inspire me. I would also like to thank the following colleagues for their advice and input on their international initiatives discussed in this book: Yvonne Bain, Judy Williams, Mandi Berry, Kari Smith, Mieke Lunenberg, Ainat Guberman, Elaine Hoter and Gerda Geerdink. Their work has been instrumental to the completion of Chapter 5 of this book. Finally – and most importantly – my love and thanks to my amazing wife, Jenny Barksfield, who patiently and critically reads all my work and for whom I have unending respect as wife, best friend, editor supreme and PSHE education champion.

FOREWORD

This volume in the series *Critical Guides for Teacher Educators* is a very significant addition. It exemplifies as much as any of the other volumes in the series exactly what it is that lies behind our intentions in offering teacher educators texts that will inform their work in a constructive and critical way.

What Gerry Czerniawski has achieved in this book is a very compelling synthesis of what is important in the working lives of teacher educators. His writing is based on extensive research – both his own and that of others – and on extensive professional experience. As has been noted, the provision of teacher education in England has become incredibly complex (Whiting et al, 2018, in press) and policy created by the government often appears to have little evidential base in research (Teacher Education Group, 2016). At the same time, as Gerry himself notes, much credibility is given to the idea of *evidence-based teaching* and indeed there has been a rapid growth of interest in teacher research.

The book helps us to understand this paradox and why it is important in the creation of new teachers. In particular, avoiding the kind of parochialism that often seems to influence policy, Gerry draws on work carried out elsewhere in the UK and internationally to show quite clearly that *it doesn't have to be like this*. He writes with such enthusiasm and passionate commitment that, rather than becoming frustrated or pessimistic about current developments in England, he exudes an optimism and a constructive approach that I believe readers will find inspiring.

To put it in his own words (from the final chapter):

The book celebrates the integrity, commitment and passion that teacher educators and teachers bring to their work and the improvements we make as we strive to improve our professional practice.

He calls for '*teacher educators [to] play a central role in re-thinking and re-defining current and future generations' conceptions of the importance and substance of both formal and informal education*'.

He readily acknowledges the variegated composition of the contemporary teacher education workforce, involving colleagues in many schools as well as in colleges and universities, and he offers advice and encouragement to all.

Ian Menter, Series Editor
Emeritus Professor of Teacher Education, University of Oxford

ABOUT THE SERIES EDITOR

Ian Menter is Emeritus Professor of Teacher Education and was formerly the Director of Professional Programmes in the Department of Education at the University of Oxford. He previously worked at the Universities of Glasgow, the West of Scotland, London Metropolitan, the West of England and Gloucestershire. Before that he was a primary school teacher in Bristol, England. His most recent publications include *A Literature Review on Teacher Education for the 21st Century* (Scottish Government) and *A Guide to Practitioner Research in Education* (Sage). His work has also been published in many academic journals.

ABOUT THE AUTHOR

Gerry Czerniawski taught humanities, business studies and sociology in schools and colleges in London before gradually moving into teaching in higher education within the political sciences and education (The Open University, University of Northampton, London Metropolitan University and London University's Institute of Education). In 2006 he joined the University of East London where he is currently Professor of Education. He has been programme leader for secondary PGCE/GTP/School Direct Humanities courses and runs the doctoral programmes in education. Gerry holds a National Teaching Fellowship from the Higher Education Academy and is a trustee and council member of the British Educational Research Association (BERA). He is the Lead Editor of The BERA Blog, Chair of the British Curriculum Forum and a Principal Fellow of the Higher Education Academy.

CHAPTER 1

INTRODUCTION: BEWARE OF THE SORCERER'S APPRENTICE!

> ## CRITICAL **ISSUES**
>
> - *To what extent can this book live up to its title?*
> - *What contexts are important when considering the work of teacher educators?*
> - *What definition best describes a teacher educator?*

Introduction

Writing a book with the title 'teacher educators in the twenty-first century' has been a daunting task – daunting, but nevertheless intensely rewarding. But if I am going to be completely honest with you, dear reader, the title is not mine but one suggested by my publisher. This places me in a slightly awkward situation, as I certainly do not want to incur their wrath (a strategically unwise course of action for any author). But as I rapidly approach my seventh decade, it is extremely unlikely that I, or indeed this book, will be around by the middle of or even the late twenty-first century, making the title's teleological foundations somewhat questionable. So, my apologies to you from the outset that I cannot fully live up to this title's promise. That said, it is a title that encourages, nay begs, a critical reflection on the state of teacher education today and the implications this current condition may have for teacher educators' future identities, professional learning, professional know-ledge, occupational position, professional values and professional impact in terms of educational research, student learning and, ultimately, societal transformation. For this book's starting point is that teacher educators are (or should be) intrinsically associated with, and championed for, the potential impact they can make in these areas.

Teacher education: a weapon of mass instruction?

Two drivers influence nation-states engaging in systemic educational reform: (i) a baffling array of metrics on the subject of learning, performance and effectiveness and (ii) the policy impact of international comparisons of educational achievement (Hargreaves, 2014, p 10). Teacher education has finally become part of their armoury. Driven by a desire to climb world rankings in educational league tables, changes in teacher training and education can be added to a list of reforms that attempt to secure greater value for money, make education systems more responsive to the requirements of industry and commerce and raise pupil achievement (Livingston and Robertson, 2001; OECD, 2010). At the supranational level, the European Commission's recent policy gaze on teacher education has led to their Education Council adopting and enacting a European agenda for improving the quality of teacher education for all countries within the European Union (European Commission, 2010, 2013, 2015). Sahlberg (2012) argues that since the 1980s, five common features of education policies and reform principles have been employed in an attempt to improve the quality of public education systems, including those associated with teacher education:

1. the standardisation of education;

2. the focus on core subjects in school (eg literacy, numeracy and science);

3. the search for low-risk ways to reach learning goals that encourage 'teaching to the test', minimising pedagogic experimentation;

4. the adoption of corporate management models as a main driver for improvement;

5. the adoption of test-based accountability for schools.

Convergence has also been said to exist around certain core themes associated with the quality of those entering the teaching profession (Hulme, 2016). These core themes include:

» the quality of entrants;

» the practicum enhancement (ie the quality of the school placement experience);

» the imperative of career-long teacher learning;

» school leadership;

» the use of evidence, including research to inform improvement (Hulme, 2016, p 37).

In this book I recognise the usefulness of identifying tendencies in policy-making at the global level but argue that, while similarity in developments of policy-making are taking place in teacher education internationally, the pace of such changes varies considerably. Ozga and Jones (2006) remind us that while *travelling policy* may be shaped by globalising trends, *embedded* policy is 'mediated by local contextual factors that may translate policy to reflect local priorities and meanings' (Ozga and Jones, 2006, p 1). I have also argued elsewhere (Czerniawski, 2010) that cultural specificities exist, which can account for the variety of ways policies are interpreted and implemented at national, regional and local levels. Nevertheless, the acknowledgement of these policy tendencies is of far-reaching importance. It is vital for those of us debating, conceptualising and developing authentic professional learning opportunities for teacher educators at a time of systemic change. It also raises questions in terms of the impact current reforms may have on future classroom pedagogic practice, what is meant by *quality* in teaching and learning and the extent to which teacher educators are suitably professionally equipped and armed for service.

The changing context of teacher education

The changing policy climate identified in the earlier discussion has meant that trends in teacher education, and the reforms associated with them, have emerged in recent years, challenging the more traditional approaches to teacher education and accelerating the time it takes to qualify as a teacher. Payne and Zeichner (2017) note that the *'traditional model of college and university-based teacher education emphasizes the knowledge of universities, or what is often termed academic knowledge'* (p 1103). While this knowledge varies depending on the length of course, type of university and its location, it has typically drawn on the disciplines of sociology, psychology, history and philosophy and been held together by pedagogical instruction and pedagogical subject knowledge (Shulman, 2015) as its epistemological glue. However, over the last decade we have witnessed a shift taking place, away from these important educational disciplines, to what some have described as a more practical and pragmatic approach to teacher education (Peiser, 2016). In countries where the marketisation of education has become a more embedded structural feature of the education system (eg in England and many parts of the United States), the number and type of teacher education providers has increased, often accompanied by the relocation of teacher preparation away from universities and into schools. The growth of Teach for America, Teach First and the Teach For All global network are powerful examples of both the rapidity and intensity of this transformation. Along with these changes to the structure and provision of teacher education, supranational organisations and national governments have placed a sharp focus on teacher quality, with policy-makers in these institutions focusing on the preparation, retention, quality and progression of teachers (OECD, 2005; Gove, 2010; European Commission, 2015). These features have, at times, been accompanied by wider international discourses reflecting the marketisation and economisation of public sector work, in which teacher education is often portrayed as a *policy problem* (Mayer, 2014).

In England this problem received particularly savage handling at the time by the incoming Secretary of State for Education, Michael Gove, with his reference to academics working and running teacher education departments in universities as *'the blob'* and *'enemies of promise'* (Gove, 2014). The implication of this derisory discourse is one in which the progressive ideas often associated with university education departments are seen to be responsible for damaging children's education. The antidote to this apparent disease and the theorisation seen as one of its symptoms has, in England, been the driver for more *school-led* teacher education with a change in direction to more on-the-job *training* (eg through School Direct and School-Centred Initial Teacher Training (SCITT)) and what some have described as the *practical turn* (Cochran-Smith, 2016). This historic bifurcation between theory and practice in initial teacher education (ITE) is well documented and remains to this day, as Murray and Mutton (2016) acknowledge:

Current understanding of ITE still all too frequently constructs a conceptual binary around 'theory/practice' and a related 'universities/schools' divide. These constructs, in tandem, position schools as the only places where 'practice' can be generated and universities as the sole 'providers' of 'theory', which is often viewed as irrelevant.

(Murray and Mutton, 2016, p 70)

However, what has been described as this practical turn and the current *perennial tension* between theory and practice (McMahon, Forde and Dickson, 2015) has also been accompanied by what some have described as a *university research turn* (Cochran-Smith, 2016). While aspects of the practical turn described here are exemplified within both the English and American teacher education systems, other education systems elsewhere have witnessed the strengthening and consolidation of higher education within initial teacher education (eg Finland, Ireland and Singapore). This consolidation can take different forms, such as efforts to relocate all initial teacher education in universities, the merging or amalgamation of teacher colleges with universities, extending the length of undergraduate and/or graduate degrees and the strengthening role of research in and on initial teacher education. However, regardless of which particular trajectory is adopted (see Chapter 5), in recent years, policy-makers have nevertheless placed a greater emphasis on the significance of the school practicum in the preparation of a future teaching workforce (European Commission, 2015). For some commentators, the implication of this emphasis for teacher educators is that *'the epistemology of teacher education has therefore changed, with experiential, practical and contemporary knowledge of teaching becoming central'* (Murray and Mutton, 2016, p 63). For those interested in understanding the professional learning of teacher educators in schools, colleges and universities, these trajectories raise questions about what professional developmental opportunities are of most value to teacher educators. But they also raise questions about the role research plays in education, its location and the extent to which teacher educators and teachers can and should (regardless of their location) be involved in educational research. Chapter 6 looks more closely at the issue of research in education and the role that teacher educators can play with particular reference to the recent British Educational Research Association in conjunction with the Royal Society for the Encouragement of Arts, Manufactures and Commerce (BERA-RSA, 2014) inquiry into educational research.

The emergence of the sorcerer's apprentice

The opening up of teacher education to market forces, deregulation and cost-cutting (Davey, 2013; Grimmet and Chinnery, 2009) has been particularly evident in England over the last couple of decades. While university and school partnerships have been a firmly embedded (and statutory) feature of teacher education since 1992, the country's schools and universities have had to navigate their way through an environment of increasing competition, ultra-accountability and external evaluation. My colleagues and I have argued elsewhere that both School Direct (SD) and SCITTs represent a significant threat to higher education institutions (HEIs) not just in terms of decreasing student numbers (and therefore income) but also the extent to which educational research remains viable within academia (Czerniawski et al, 2018). McNamara and Murray (2013) also argue that SD and the wider reforms that accompany these developments are radical in that they combine three elements:

1. *an ideologically driven understanding of teaching as essentially only a craft rather than a complex and fundamentally intellectual activity;*

2. *an apprenticeship model of teacher training that can be located entirely in the workplace;*

3. *the related and highly questionable assumption that a longer period of time spent in schools inevitably – and unproblematically – leads to better and more relevant student learning.*

(McNamara and Murray, 2013, p 14)

While I am no fan of conservative approaches to education in general, uncertainty and incoherence in teacher education can create spaces into which overly simplistic definitions of teaching as *craft*, teacher knowledge as *practical* and teacher education as an *apprenticeship* can and do emerge. A report from the British Educational Research Association in conjunction with the Royal Society for the Encouragement of Arts, Manufactures and Commerce (BERA-RSA, 2014) highlights the importance of *research engagement*, ie the involvement of teachers and educational leaders in carrying out research and *research literacy*, ie that teachers should be

familiar with a range of research methods, with the latest research findings and with the implications of this research for day-to-day practice, and for education policy and practice more broadly.

(BERA-RSA, 2014, p 40)

As we consider the professional learning and professional development of teacher educators in this book, it is worth remembering that the sorcerer's apprentice found himself in deep water through mimicking the actions of his master [sic] without the requisite skills, knowledge and attributes developed over time with rigour, scholarship and practice.

And finally ... who exactly are teacher educators?

After all these years, and despite the transformation taking place in teacher education that we have briefly looked at in this introduction, I still like Clarke's (2001) definitions of terms in teacher education for their simplicity (in the best deployment of the word):

A profession: an occupation requiring advanced instruction in a specialised field of study prior to certification;

Teaching: the professional practice of engaging learners in the construction of knowing directly related to a particular area of study;

A teacher: someone for whom teaching is a significant part of his or her professional practice and daily responsibility;

Teacher education: the professional practice of engaging teachers in the construction of knowledge directly related to the area of study known as 'teaching';

Teacher educator: someone for whom teacher education is a significant part of his or her professional practice and daily responsibility.

(Clarke, 2001, p 600)

The difficulty I have with Clarke's fifth and final definition is that many teacher educators today find themselves working in more elaborate, often more competitive, working environments than those he was considering at the time of writing. As seen in Chapter 2, the variability in teacher educators' work roles is well documented and can include teaching, coaching, the facilitation of collaboration between diverse organisations and stakeholders, assessment, gatekeeping (into the teaching profession), curriculum development, marketing, research, critical inquiry and writing (Lunenberg, Dengerink and Korthagen, 2014; Swennen, Jones and Volman, 2010). In this book I have therefore opted for a definition of teacher educators used here as an inclusive term to encompass *all* who are professionally engaged in the initial and ongoing education of teachers, including those who work in universities, colleges and schools.

IN A **NUTSHELL**

This chapter has given a brief overview of recent policy developments within teacher education and the implications of these developments for teacher educators. In Chapter 2, I introduce the concept of identity before examining more closely how this concept has been applied to teacher educators. Chapter 3 identifies existing research on the professional learning needs of teacher educators and how these needs might vary depending on the context in which teacher educators are situated (eg school, university, Anglophone/non-Anglophone countries). Chapter 4 introduces some general discussions about what is meant by *knowledge* before looking at how some themes within these discussions have been applied to the knowledge of teachers and teacher educators. Acknowledging significant shifts in how teacher education is conceptualised, designed and delivered, Chapter 5 introduces Cochran-Smith's (2016) five *turns* in teacher education worthy of mention when considering international developments within this field. The chapter then looks briefly at initiatives from Australia, Norway, the Netherlands and Scotland as well as the work of the International Forum for Teacher Educator Development (InFo-TED). Chapter 6 discusses the complex and often contested relationship between research-based knowledge and scholarship and how both can inform the professional learning of teacher educators. Finally, Chapter 7 draws together the key themes identified in the book and how these themes can be used to inform the authentic induction and professional learning of all teacher educators.

REFLECTIONS ON **CRITICAL ISSUES**

Attempting to write a book for *all* who are professionally engaged in the initial and ongoing education of teachers is laced with pitfalls. Making generalisations about teacher educators' experience is problematic, despite existing trends in the implementation of professional standards' frameworks, and, in some cases, the increasing take-up of school-based and school-driven teacher education (White, Dickerson and Weston, 2015). As Chapter 2 demonstrates, universities, colleges and schools differ in their teacher education programmes; and university, college and school departments may vary in their interpretations of the knowledge, skills, practices, ethics, values and attributes that different frameworks prioritise. This means that the book has many limitations that I acknowledge from the outset. I would, for example, have wished to devote significantly more pages to the work of teacher educators working in schools and further education (FE). Nevertheless, I hope that this text introduces you to ideas that you can take forward and use critically to inform your own professional development and professional learning and of those whom you teach, train and educate.

CRITICAL **ISSUES**

- *To what extent is it possible or desirable to use the term* identity *when collectively referring to teacher educators?*
- *What is the relationship between teacher educators' identities and their professional roles?*
- *How might an understanding of this relationship provide the foundations for the professional learning of teacher educators?*

Introduction

In this chapter I introduce you to aspects of the literature on identity, significant not just to professional learning but for a wider commitment to the efficacy of teacher education in general. This point is reinforced by McAnulty and Cuenca (2014, p 36):

The identities of teacher educators help shape their dispositions and commitments to certain norms within a teacher education program. If we assume that the overall experience of a teacher education programme is intimately tied to the ways in which teacher educators enact these dispositions, then identity development should be of critical concern.

The chapter starts by looking at the concept of identity before examining more closely how and why, within the literature on teacher education, this concept has been applied to teacher educators. Acknowledging the rapidly changing context of teacher education both nationally and internationally, it then looks more closely at *boundary crossing* and how, as a concept, it can contribute to understanding the challenges faced by teacher educators working in or crossing into new institutions. Finally, the chapter looks at the identity work carried out by teacher educators working in schools amidst what has been described as a '*practicum turn in teacher education*' (Mattsson, Eilertson and Rorrison, 2011, p 17).

What do we mean by identity?

Identity is one of those terms we use all the time without necessarily thinking about its meaning. In common parlance the term is often used interchangeably with *personality*, although both concepts are embedded in different disciplines (the former primarily associated with sociology, anthropology and cultural studies and the latter most frequently with psychology). However, no one universally accepted concept of identity exists, either in the social sciences or teacher education, and it would be impossible within the confines of this chapter to detail this contested field of writing. Essentialist understandings of the concept can, for example, '*assume a unique core or essence to identity which remain more or less the same throughout life*' (Marshall, 1998, p 294). In contrast, some post-modern views acknowledge the concept's fluidity, stating that

as the possibility of a single secure identity, inherited at birth and developed within a personal and social narrative of progress, disappears over the horizon along with the utopias that such a possibility suggests could exist, the notion of identity as a construct … gathers pace.

(Davidson, 2000, p 1)

In this chapter I have therefore been selective rather than being exhaustive and have chosen explanations deemed useful when considering the term's significance in relation to what Izadinia (2014) describes as the '*newly emerging concept of teacher educator identity*' (p 426).

Teacher educator is used here as an inclusive term to encompass all who are professionally engaged in the initial and ongoing education of teachers, including those who work in universities, colleges and schools. A number of reviews have been done exploring the literature on teacher educators' identity (see Swennen, Jones and Volman, 2010; Williams, Ritter and Bullock, 2012; Izadinia, 2014). By *teacher educator identity* I refer to how teacher educators view themselves; how they view others with whom they engage professionally (eg other colleagues, student teachers, policy-makers, publishers, etc); and how they believe others might perceive them. This conception of identity, while not exhaustive, draws attention to its multiple and fluid dimensions of what Beauchamp and Thomas (2009) refer to as '*how to be*', '*how to act*' and '*how to understand*' the profession (ibid, p 178). It acknowledges the complex interaction between personal identities (eg those associated with class, gender, race and self-image) and professional identities. And it recognises the often painful reconciliation process experienced by many teacher educators as they shed their former identity as a *teacher* and develop their novice identity as a *teacher educator*.

Professional identities are social identities in that they are a fusion of both the personal identity of the teacher educator – ie the image of their own qualifications, characteristics and values – and a collective identity – ie the experience of being an integrated part of a group (Ulriksen, 1995). Collectively, professional identity may be seen as developing in response to socio-cultural values, workplace discourses, practices and norms as understood and contested within any occupational group (Izidinia, 2014). However, differences in the constellations and configurations of influence and different patterns of working relationships, in conjunction with different personal histories and values, ensure that the development of teacher educators' identities is likely to differ significantly for different individuals within and beyond what may appear on the surface, in broadly similar professional contexts and/or settings. Given the diversity and contestation within and across this occupational grouping, such differences therefore make it problematic to define its collective identity.

Why is teacher educator identity important?

Professional identities form a key part of teacher educators' ways of understanding the world of teacher education as well as the ways in which they enact their beliefs, values and principles through work. The exploration of identity is therefore part of a wider commitment to promoting the understanding and improvement of teacher education in general.

The European Commission's recent policy gaze on teacher education has led to their Education Council adopting and enacting an European agenda for improving the quality of teacher education in all countries within the European Union (European Commission, 2010, 2013, 2015). While this agenda (despite *Brexit*) is to be welcomed, it poses difficulties for those conceptualising and developing critically authentic professional learning opportunities for teacher educators. While the supply chain to a university-based teacher education in many countries draws from the school sector, there are notable exceptions, eg in Finland, where teacher educators are recruited mainly from the field of higher education rather than from schools (Hökkä, 2012). Cochran-Smith (2003) has argued that before the professional development of teacher educators can be taken seriously, their identities have to be defined. However, defining teacher educators as an occupational group and making generalisations about the work they do is challenging, not least because the enterprise of teacher education is often understood differently within and across members of this group locally, nationally and internationally.

Teacher educators' identities and the institutional settings in which these identities are activated are mutually constitutive. Drawing on one interpretation, identity embodies '*a shifting amalgam of personal biography, culture, social influence and institutional values which may change according to role and circumstance*' (Day et al, 2006, p 613). While a teacher educator's role is not synonymous with their identity (Britzman, 1992), their day-to-day professional activities inform that identity in a process that is reliant on social interaction in a range of socio-cultural groupings. The significance of this relationship between identity, learning and the workplace is captured in Wenger's (1998) use of the phrase '*communities of practice*'. By becoming a member of a new professional community and taking part in the social practices associated with that community, new identities are constructed as new types of learning bring about a change in the learner. But the nature of this learning and its relationship to teacher educator identity is far from clear. Murray's (2002) pioneering work on teacher educator identity conceptualises teacher educators as *second order practitioners* involved in the processes of (re)production of the discourses of the *first order field* of schooling. Here, complex processes of identity play out with teachers as *first order practitioners*, mentors as practising school teachers and school-based teacher educators move *between first and second order practice,* depending on whether they are teaching children/young people or mentoring pre-service teachers.

The fear of transition

Murray (2014) draws attention to how occupational change for neophyte teacher educators, usually those coming from a background in school teaching to higher education (HE), can bring with it professional uncertainty and shifts in identity. Relatively poorly conceived university induction programmes for new staff often compound this transition, particularly for those coming from the more practitioner-based occupations such as teaching, nursing and social work. Four transitional fears have been identified in the literature by Braund (2015) as teacher educators move into university employment:

1. uncertainty with new professional roles (Boyd and Harris, 2010);

2. the nature of adult pedagogy (Murray and Male, 2005; Loughran, 2006);

3. fears in relation to the adequacy of professional and academic knowledge bases (McKeon and Harrison, 2010);

4. the relative absence of collaborative working environments to facilitate reflective workplace learning (Eraut, 2004; Harrison and McKeon, 2008).

Such occupational changes can be particularly challenging for those coming from often senior positions within schools. Once they are in university employment, many teacher educators find themselves in relatively lower hierarchical positions in a university department and working within a discipline (education) often considered to be low status, soft, applied and marginalised (Becher and Trowler, 2002; Murray, 2014).

Variability in the work of teacher educators

The variability in teacher educators' work roles is well documented (Lunenberg, Dengerink and Korthagen, 2014; Swennen, Jones and Volman, 2010) and can include teaching, coaching, the facilitation of collaboration between diverse organisations and stakeholders, assessment, gatekeeping (into the teaching profession), curriculum development, research, critical inquiry and writing. The nature of these roles will vary depending on a number of factors such as the nature of employment (eg part time/full time, length of contract or length of time in service), the phase (eg primary/secondary/post-16) and whether teacher educators are situated in schools, colleges or universities. However, it is the scholar and researcher roles that have been cited as being the most pressing concern for novice teacher educators (Boyd, Harris and Murray, 2011; Braund, 2015).

Griffiths, Thompson and Hryniewicz (2014) make a further distinction between two groups of university-based teacher educators. Teacher educators coming from Anglophone countries often move to universities having previously taught in schools, but in other countries teacher educators are drawn mainly from academic disciplines and often lack practical teaching experience (Griffiths, Thompson and Hryniewicz, 2014). Both groups are likely to encounter different transitional experiences and tensions in the development of their own professional identities and their subsequent learning needs. One such tension can emerge as they navigate and evaluate their career trajectories through institutional norms and expectations while encountering colleagues who embrace their identity as either a researcher or a teacher educator. Both identities may, to varying degrees, be bolstered or deflated by accountability frameworks associated with national and international rankings pressure on universities.

The complex nature of professional identity work

Much of Goffman's (1959) work focused on the micro-political nature of everyday life for which he has adopted a *dramaturgical approach*, comparing social life to the theatre.

He argues that individuals are social actors following *scripts* and adopting roles to give performances. While the scripts may well be written for us, we nevertheless have choice (ie agency) to revise and interpret them in any way we desire, subject to the discourses that are available to us. Viewed through this perspective, professional identity work is complex, not least because how teacher educators *perform* their identities will be contingent, at least in part, on the ways in which they position themselves and are positioned by those significant in their professional lives (eg colleagues within a department, within the faculty, within professional networks, etc). These significations will vary locally and nationally. Being a teacher educator is fundamentally an emotional endeavour and subject to the powerful ethics of care (Noddings, 1992) that many teacher educators would have brought with them from their former roles as teachers. This endeavour is situated within wider national and international discourses reflecting the marketisation of public sector work and the development, in many places, of an audit culture in which the performance of professionals and institutions is increasingly measured by externally determined targets (Apple, 2005; Wilkins and Wood, 2009). As universities increasingly encounter pervasive auditing and accountability frameworks (eg the Research Excellence Framework (REF) and the Teaching Excellence Framework (TEF) in England), one might mull over the extent to which cultures of performativity in higher education (Ball, 2012) erode those ethics of care as certain identities are invoked, revoked, performed or grappled with – most notably those associated with being a teacher, counsellor, mentor, researcher or gatekeeper to the teaching profession.

Davey helpfully divides international empirical studies on the professional identity of teacher educators into three groups:

1. *studies of the demographics of teacher educators in higher education as a particular disciplinary community or occupational sub-group;*

2. *studies of the impact of managerialist reformism in tertiary education policy on the work and lives of academics generally;*

3. *case studies and self-studies from individual teacher educators relating their own experience of the practice of teacher education.*

(Davey, 2013, p 19)

In self-studies of teacher educators, individual professional identity is often defined as the *practitioner* identity and is therefore integrally related to individual constructions of practice within the social space(s) of teacher education which each individual inhabits (eg WIlliams, 2013; Newbury, 2014). The role of these social spaces in the construction of identity is important, as we shall see in the next section.

Teacher educators as boundary crossers

Entering employment as a university teacher educator and *academic* for the first time can be an exciting, challenging and bewildering experience. The reconstruction process of pedagogy and identity as *expert teachers* become teacher educators in academia has been well documented (Murray and Male, 2005; Boyd and Harris, 2010) – a process referred to in this chapter as boundary crossing.

Suchman (1994) used the term *boundary crossing* to refer to the challenges faced by professionals when entering new and unfamiliar employment. Earlier we identified two groups of teacher educators working in universities – those coming from predominantly disciplinary research backgrounds and those who are former school and/or college teachers. Both groups, at least initially, are likely to be juggling different combinations of professional capital (Hargreaves and Fullan, 2012) during the course of that transition. For example, while those in the first group may not have direct experience, knowledge and understanding about how schools work, they will possess high levels of scholarly capital including research expertise. Teacher educators coming from a school-based background, on the other hand, may lack these particular research skills but are likely to possess a more situated understanding of teachers, their professional environment, pedagogic competence (albeit with a younger demographic) and leadership. The challenges both groups face as fledgling teacher educators may vary. The partnership and relationship maintenance (Ellis et al, 2013) required when visiting student/trainee teachers on school placements will present significantly different sets of challenges for those whose professional background has been largely forged within research trajectories in comparison to university staff who were former teachers. Similarly the requirements to research and write articles as an academic may be extremely daunting for those who have held senior positions in schools but have never necessarily published anything.

A third space for identity construction

Akkerman and Bakker's (2011) synthesis of 181 studies on boundary crossing, spanning health care, technology, science and teaching point to four mechanisms of learning (identification, coordination, reflection and transformation) as people move from and between different professional contexts. This learning encompasses *'new understandings, identity development, change of practices and institutional development'* (p 142). Bain, Dengerink and Gray (2017) note that boundary crossing is closely related with cultural-historical activity theory (Engeström, 2005) whereby two *activity systems* interact to construct shared in-between spaces of practices that can provide rich personal and professional learning. Some writers (see Bullock, 2012; Williams, 2013) have pointed to this *third space* of identity construction existing between university and school-based teacher educators. In her own self-study, Williams (2013) notes that

[t]he boundary practices of the third space require a delicate balancing act of acknowledging and respecting the personal and professional identities of all involved, and using dialogue to facilitate professional learning conversations.

(p 128)

This hybrid space crosses both academic and practitioner boundaries and rejects some of the artificial binaries (eg practitioner and academic knowledge, theory and practice, etc) constituted therein (Darling-Hammond, 2010; Zeichner, 2010). In such spaces, Korthagen, Loughran and Russell (2006) suggest teacher educators hold *'three different perspectives simultaneously: the perspective of the individual learning to teach, the perspective of the teacher in a school and the perspective of the teacher in the university setting'* (p 1034). This polycontextuality (Kidd, 2012) can both inform and enrich the professional identity, knowledge and pedagogy associated with being a teacher educator. But it can also pose further challenges for those entering teacher education for the first time. As boundary crossers, teacher educators are often members of different horizontally segregated communities of disciplinary practice, eg those associated with mathematics, history and drama. The professional values held within these communities may have distinctly different conceptions of what makes up appropriate knowledge, pedagogy and profes-sional practice and even what determines a good teacher in the first place. Writing about the challenges associated with the journey from teacher to teacher educator, Williams and Ritter (2010, p 90) note that

[o]ne identity is not discarded in favor of the other ... but utilized in ways that will help former classroom teachers to 'repackage' who they are as teachers ... [This] raises questions about how novice teacher educators can be initiated into the profession in ways that support their transition from school teaching to teaching teachers in the academic con-text, and contributes to the on-going reconstruction of their professional identities.

The coalescing of boundary domains within a third space in teacher education is a process that can provide invaluable opportunities for professional critical reflection and transform-ation. However, bringing together professionals with different skill domains and providing an opportunity for brokering boundary-crossing activities can be challenging and will often be dependent on the institutional context. But it's worth it as these shared in-between spaces of practices can provide enormous potential for rich personal and professional learning.

School-based teacher educators

So far we have looked at teacher educators working in HE. However, not all teacher educators work in universities. In some countries, most notably in England, the prevalence of school-centred teacher education is increasing and, while still in its infancy, a growing body of literature exists that explores the identity and identity work of this particular occu-pational grouping (Darling-Hammond and Lieberman, 2012; White, 2013; Swennen, 2014; Amott, 2016).

The work of teacher educators in schools (in addition to their dual role as school teachers) tends to focus on the professional learning of two groups – student/trainee teachers and more experienced teachers who are engaged in their own continuing professional develop-ment (CPD). In England, for example, school-based teacher educators will often be tasked with the responsibility of organising some or all aspects of both strands of professional learning for both pre-service and in-service teachers. This work can include the recruitment of trainee teachers, the design, implementation and evaluation of course components, and the assessments at the end of the training/CPD processes (White, Dickerson and

Weston, 2015; McNamara, Murray and Phillips, 2017). Models vary but many school-based educators will work independently and/or with private providers and/or networks of schools while others will work with universities and HEI-based teacher educators. While teacher educators working in schools do not necessarily face some of the expectations that their university counterparts experience (eg the same pressures to carry out research, publish findings etc), they do share many features of the dual identity work discussed in this chapter. They are, for example, simultaneously both first and second order practitioners (Murray, 2002), ie both teachers and teacher educators. And yet schools are also complex and often hectic institutions that have structurally developed over time to prioritise pupil learning over that of the professional learning of teachers and teacher educators. Schools are not as large as universities and therefore do not necessarily have parity of access to the professional networks and communities of practice that HEI-based teacher educators have (eg those associated with research, publications, conferences etc.).

However, in what has been described as a *pendulum swing* away from the dominance of HEIs towards a greater role for schools and teachers in the formation of beginning teachers (Murray and Mutton, 2016; Mutton, Burn and Menter, 2017), the rapid transformation of the education system in England serves to not only problematise simplistic descriptive bifurcations of school- and university-based teacher educators but the very purpose of primary, secondary and tertiary education. This swing is part of a wider '*practicum turn in teacher education*' (Mattsson, Eilertson and Rorrison, 2011, p 17) acknowledged as an international phenomenon in which many countries are increasing the school experi-ence in initial teacher preparation (Darling-Hammond and Lieberman, 2012; Mutton, Burn and Menter, 2017). In England the growth of employment-based routes into teaching over the last two decades (eg the Graduate Teacher Programme and Schools Direct initiatives in England) has been accompanied by diversity and fragmentation within the profession. Even as the roles available for HE-based teacher educators in workplace learning have diminished, the importance of mentoring roles for pre-service teachers in schools has steadily grown (Murray, Czerniawski and Kidd, 2013) along with the pressures on teachers in schools to market, capture and facilitate elements of a fragmenting teacher education system.

The growth of academy chains (in England) has been accompanied by a renewed interest in school-based practitioner research recently accelerated in 2016 by the growth of research schools set up in partnership with the Education Endowment Foundation (EEF), the Institute for Effective Education (IEE) and backed by the Department for Education (DfE). The intention is for such schools to be '*recognized as leaders in bridging the gap between education research and everyday classroom practice*' (EEF, 2017). While it is too soon to give a clear indication as to the effects such schools will have on the education system, their existence further complicates clear-cut distinctions between the roles and identities of teacher educators. The emergence of new research related to job roles in schools (eg Research Leads and Research Advocates) and the rise of grassroots teacher-led organisations, eg researchED, also raises important questions around the purpose of educational research and who, why and how and for whom it is carried out.

IN A **NUTSHELL**

The identities of teacher educators have long been described as Janus-like and schizophrenic in an acknowledgement of their multiple roles as *'school person, scholar, researcher, methodologist and visitor to a strange planet'* (Ducharme and Judge, 1993, p 4). Over three decades later this description has startling contemporary relevancy to this boundary-crossing profession. Far from neat and tidy, all professional identity work is prone to the *'idiosyncratic nature of people and the myriad and flowing situations in which they exist'* (Gaudelli and Ousley, 2009, p 932). How teacher educators perform their identities (Santorro, 2009) will be contingent on the ways in which they position themselves and are positioned by those significant in their professional lives. These considerations and significations will vary locally, nationally and regionally.

By understanding, more fully, the sorts of transitional dilemmas encountered by those entering teacher education for the first time, institutional leadership teams in schools, colleges and universities are in a position to construct more meaningful professional induction and more sustained, valued, authentic and nuanced professional learning opportunities. And it is to the topic of teacher educators' professional learning that this book will now turn to in the next chapter.

REFLECTIONS ON **CRITICAL ISSUES**

- *Research carried out by the International Forum for Teacher Educator Development (InFo-TED) on the professional learning needs of teacher educators (Czerniawski, Guberman and MacPhail, 2017) indicates that teacher educators want to be part of a collaborative community where they can feel supported, listened to and share their practices and experiences. However, the enterprise of teacher education can be understood differently within and across different members of that occupational group, locally, nationally and internationally. Do these variations make it problematic to define a collective identity for teacher educators, given this diversity and contestation within and across the group?*

- *If the supply chain for many university teacher education departments draws increasingly from schools, how might greater awareness of research on the identities and professional learning of teacher educators be used by universities to inform a more enlightened and structured academic induction period for teacher educators entering university employment for the first time?*

CRITICAL **ISSUES**

- *To what extent is it possible to draw a distinction between* continuing professional development *and* professional learning?
- *How does workplace learning literature enrich our understanding of teacher educators?*
- *What professional learning activities do teacher educators value and find most effective?*

Introduction

Professional development, continuing professional development (CPD) and *professional learning* are concepts very often conflated in meaning despite many writers defining these terms differently. While the body of literature relating these concepts to teacher educators is still in its infancy, it is beginning to gather momentum (White, Dickerson and Weston, 2015; Murray, Lunenberg and Smith, 2017; Van der Klink et al, 2017). In this chapter I examine select studies from this literature and the opportunities it offers teacher educators to consider how best they can develop their professional expertise. This is important, not least because of the European Commission's (2013) report, *Supporting Teacher Educators for Better Learning Outcomes*, which has acknowledged the relative lack of support given to teacher educators at the start of their professional careers:

Since there is no initial training for teacher educators and only limited induction, opportunities for teacher educators to reflect and to develop their professional qualities throughout their careers are extremely important. These learning opportunities should respond to individual professional needs, but also prepare them for new developments in (teacher) learning, (teacher) education, the teaching profession and society.

(Smith, 2003)

The chapter begins by looking closely at what we mean by *professional development* and *professional learning*, and how both terms vary in their significance for teacher educators. It examines the literature on professional learning in the workplace and how it can contribute to increasing our understanding about the professional learning needs and preferences of teacher educators in both universities and schools.

Professional development: more than just a portmanteau term

Professional development is often deployed as a portmanteau term for what Day and Sachs (2004) describe as a *'hugely complex intellectual and emotional endeavour'* (p 4). Typically, activities cited include observations, on-the-job coaching and mentoring, team teaching, self-directed study, in-service courses, sabbaticals, membership of working groups and networks, collaborative learning (both formally and informally), professional reflection and research (Dymoke and Harrison, 2006; Bates, Swennen and Jones, 2011; Czerniawski, Guberman and MacPhail, 2017). However, writing about teachers, Stoll and Earl (2011, p 4) draw a distinction between professional development and professional learning:

Both are intentional, ongoing, systematic processes. Over time, however, the term 'professional development' has taken on connotations of delivery of some kind of information … in order to influence their practice whereas 'professional learning' implies an internal process in which individuals create professional knowledge through interaction with this information in a way that challenges previous assumptions and creates new meanings.

Despite the growing body of literature on teacher educators' professional learning, this area of study is still relatively under-researched, with much of the literature drawing on teachers' continuing professional development (CPD) in schools. Kennedy (2005), for example, has identified nine models of teachers' CPD in international literature, classified in relation to their capacity for supporting professional autonomy and transformative practice. These teacher-based models have been usefully applied to literature on teacher educators' professional learning and development (see Bates, Swennen and Jones 2011).

» *Training model*: Delivered by experts to passive learners, this model is a top-down, skills-based technocratic view of professional development, eg early models of mentor training in which school mentors attended sessions run by university-based teacher educators that were often held at the university.

» *Award-bearing model*: Award-bearing programmes normally validated by higher education institutions (HEIs) are deployed in this model, eg master's level programmes.

» *Deficit model*: This model positions professional development needs arising from becoming a teacher educator and acted upon either by the individual or part of a managed process on the part of the employer institution.

» *Cascade model*: In this model, an individual attends a professional learning event and then re-presents the content and resources of the event to other colleagues.

» *Standards-based model*: This model is based on the use of standards (sometimes described as professional frameworks) for teacher educators (eg as used in the Netherlands and the United States). Debates exist as to what extent these standards might be imposed on or owned by teacher educators and the extent to which they are seen as rules or guidelines accordingly.

» *Coaching model*: This model emphasises the ways in which novice teacher educators work alongside more established members of the professional community or communities of practice (Lave and Wenger, 1991).

» *Community of practice model*: Acknowledging many aspects of the coaching model above, this model emphasises the importance of legitimate peripheral participation (Lave and Wenger, 1991). The importance of supportive relationships in engaging with the practices of the community is emphasised. By engaging in peripheral activities, new entrants become socialised into the tasks, ways-of-being, terminology and organising principles of the community.

» *Action research model*: With its focus on reflective practice, this model places high value on research engagement as a process in professional learning. While not demeaning the value of externally produced research the emphasis is on teacher educators identifying and implementing their own research activity.

» *Transformative model*: Aligning professional learning to educational change, this model effectively enables an opportunity to combine some or all of the above models, positioning CPD as an opportunity to support and promote whole scale change in the education system.

Hadar and Brody (2017) divide professional learning programmes and models into two paths. The first, self-guided learning, consists of teacher educators engaging in research (often self-study) individually or in groups (see Vanassche and Kelchtermans's 2015 review of teacher educators' self-study literature). The second path consists of more formalised programmes, courses and events specifically designed for teacher educators. The authors sub-divide this second classification into (a) programmes initiated by associations for teacher educators (see Chapter 5) that serve the needs of teacher educators from different institutions and (b) specific institutions providing in-service programmes of learning for their own employees (see below). This bifurcation is helpful when considering a further distinction made by Lipowski et al (2011) between two forms of professional learning:

1. *In-service programmes* are organised formal programmes for practitioners within the institutions where they work, considered by some to be the primary way in which they receive continuing support (Loucks-Horsley et al, 1997).

2. *Continuous experiential learning* accommodates the more informal learning opportunities that contribute to everyday professional practice, the importance of which cannot and should not be underestimated when trying to understand the work teacher educators do in different national locations and the professional support they need (MacPhail et al, 2014). It is to the informal learning that takes place in the workplace that we now turn our attention.

Understanding professional learning in the workplace

In the introduction to their book on workplace learning in teacher education, McNamara, Murray and Jones (2014) draw attention to the historical trajectory England has taken in terms of workplace learning. This is a trajectory that has shifted from the nineteenth-century classroom-based apprenticeship model of teacher education to the more theory-laden university-based model broadly adopted by the second half of the twentieth century. However, since the 1990s the authors point to the turning of the tide in England (in contrast to much of the rest of Europe) with a return to a more extensive workplace-based model of teacher education, fuelled by *radical ideological fervour* (ibid, p 1). But the authors also point out that this relocation of professional learning to the classroom is one that is qualitatively different and more complex than its nineteenth-century ancestor, and that as such, it makes England an interesting test-bed for understanding the complexities in workplace learning.

The body of literature associated with workplace and practice-based professional learning frameworks continues to grow, but its capacity for theorising such learning is still relatively under-deployed within the literature on teacher educators. As we saw earlier, Lave and Wenger's (1991) concepts of communities of practice and situated learning have dominated much of this literature. Both authors argue that this type of learning involves participation in a community of practice with learning moving from legitimate peripheral participation to central participation within that community. For example, I might start my new job at a university knowing what to teach, but it might take me several weeks to know who to talk to, who to avoid, where to sit, the informal and formal rules, norms and values I should adhere to if I am to be accepted as a colleague within that professional community. Communities of practice are made up of individuals who mutually engage in an activity and develop communal resources over a period of time. Learning in this sense is about participating in the practices associated with that community rather than an acquisition of knowledge per se. Learning is situated within the practices and social cultural context of that community (eg a university department, school, publishing company, etc). A community is viewed as *'the social configuration in which our enterprises are defined as worth pursuing and our participation is recognizable as competence'* (Wenger, 1998, p 5). Legitimate peripheral participation describes how novice employees start by engaging with subordinate and auxiliary practices within the periphery of that community (eg understanding the protocols of school visits; who to go to for important information within the department, etc). As novices gain more experience, they move towards the central participation within that community (eg being able to design and facilitate a curriculum for student teachers). Understanding the significance of different communities of practice within any organisation is significant not just in providing greater insight into how individuals develop professionally but how communities of practice can contribute to the development of larger organisations (eg universities) of which they are a part (Philpott, 2014).

Knowledge for, in and of practice

In discussing teachers' professional practice-based learning, Cochran-Smith and Lytle (1999) distinguish between knowledge-*for*-practice, knowledge-*in*-practice and knowledge-*of*-practice. The authors conceive knowledge *for* practice as the formal substantive content knowledge required for teachers to improve their own practice and the learning of their students. The assumption here being that this formal knowledge generated by university-based researchers leads to more effective teaching and learning. Knowledge *in* practice focuses on the day-to-day practical knowledge of the teacher '*embedded in practice and in teachers' reflections on practice*' (Cochran-Smith and Lytle, 1999, p 250). This knowledge can be enhanced by reflecting on the work of expert colleagues and the challenging situations encountered every day at work. By focusing on knowledge in practice educators are encouraged to be aware and challenge their own assumptions, reasoning and decision making. Knowledge *of* practice assumes that knowledge to teach well is generated when teachers treat their own classrooms and schools '*as sites for intentional investigation*' while treating the knowledge produced by others as '*generative material for interrogation and interpretation*' (Cochran-Smith and Lytle, 1999, p 250). Practice-based education (PBE) locates learning in all three of these domains, acknowledging their interrelationship and significance in the process of professional reflection. In this reconceptualisation of the reflective practitioner (Schön 1983), PBE embraces a '*form of social practice which shapes the educational development of individuals, framed around a perspective, model or theory of education that encompasses interactive philosophical, political, moral, technical and practical dimensions*' (Higgs, 2011, p 9). For the teacher educator, this emphasis on the complexity, value and significance of this type of reflection adds further weight to the distinction made earlier between teacher training and teacher education. It also adds weight to the argument that there is '*an urgent need to re-affirm teachers' and teacher educators' professionalism in terms of a research-based profession*' (Jones et al, 2011, p 272).

What professional learning activities do university-based teacher educators value?

As we have seen in the previous chapter, the transition from teacher to teacher educator is not something that happens immediately. Moving into university employment for the first time can leave many experienced teachers feeling deskilled, isolated and insecure about the expectations of their performance as novice university employees (Labaree, 2003; van Helzen et al, 2011). As teachers they had one career – working within a relatively small organisation, ie the school (or college) that employed them. Writing about early career researchers, Laudel and Glaser (2008) argue that the job of being an academic, working in large organisations like universities, actually consists of three (not one) interrelated but largely independent careers:

1. a cognitive career – ie the development of a research trail and knowledge base (made up of published articles, grants, bids, etc);

2. a community career – developed through the participation in the knowledge production and academic communities associated with their discipline (eg reviewing journal articles for publishers; membership of subject associations; editorial teams, etc);

3. an organisational career – the specific performance expectations of the employer institution (eg the career path as identified by the university job specification).

Laudel and Glaser (2008) argue that the nature of these three careers, and the fact that much of the work that goes into the development of a community career rather than directly associated with the employer organisation, accounts for why many academics feel decoupled from their employer organisation. It is not surprising then that Murray and Male (2005) have argued that novice teacher educators can take up to three years to acclimatise to the expectations, roles and forms of professional knowledge associated with working in higher education. The nature of this transition to central participation in these communities of practice, and its significance for the facilitation of meaningful professional induction into the organisation and the professional, cannot be underestimated.

A recent international study (Czerniawski, Guberman and MacPhail, 2017) of higher education-based teacher educators suggests that many teacher educators are only moderately satisfied with their experiences of induction and professional development. The study provided an international and comparative needs analysis through a survey of 1158 higher education-based teacher educators in the countries participating in the International Forum for Teacher Educator Development (InFo-TED): Belgium, Ireland, Israel, the Netherlands, Norway and the UK. Participants in the study were asked to choose the professional learning opportunities that would most effectively address their identified needs. The following five were deemed the most effective at addressing those needs.

1. More availability of time

The tasks most frequently identified as requiring more time were related to engaging in scholarly activity such as reading and conducting research, academic writing and time to think and develop ideas. There were suggestions that institutions should provide a realistic time allocation to research-related activities. Other tasks requiring more time that would contribute to teacher educators' more general professional learning included reading widely across disciplines, discussions with colleagues on teaching practices, values and philosophies as well as on the incorporation of new programmes and their associated pedagogies.

2. Research skills

Teacher educators commented on their need to develop their research skills in the areas of writing, research methodology and methods, research ethics and data analysis. Professional learning needs were identified at two levels. The first level was made up of how to conduct research and develop a research portfolio; how to access and engage in small-scale research; how to write for the right journals; and how to locate conferences and integrate research into their lectures. A second level related to those who wished to extend their research profile to international audiences as well as contribute to country-specific research exercise frameworks.

3. Use of ICT/online learning/social media

The third most frequent professional learning need focused on how best to use digital technologies for enhanced teaching and learning. Online learning and associated materials were mentioned, with an interest in teaching platforms that integrate online materials into everyday teaching. Social networking and social media were also mentioned as forums through which teacher educators believed they could support teaching and student learning. By far the most frequent response to how best to address the professional learning need of using ICT and related practices was the need for more courses and training workshops.

4. Publish research/academic writing

The need to publish research and/or write for publication was noted at two levels. The first was in relation to those participants who conveyed the need to begin writing for publication, seeking direction on how best to develop ideas and subsequently transform ideas into a publication, as well as understanding more about the publishing process. The second level came from those participants identifying themselves as having experience in publishing, but who wanted to increase their publication rate, develop a higher quality of publication and consider how to write for different audiences (eg policy-makers, grant-assessment boards). Coaching and mentoring were closely followed by collaborating with more experienced colleagues as suggestions on how best to address these needs.

5. Consideration of pedagogical principles/delivery

Participants were explicit in their specific needs related to pedagogy. These included upskilling in new pedagogies associated with particular subject disciplines, and developing more generic teaching and learning strategies (eg active teaching approaches, the integration of theory and practice, self-directed learning and assessment and feedback). The role pedagogy can play in effective class management (eg managing large class sizes, managing different learning needs, managing different populations such as socially and economically disadvantaged students) was also prioritised. University courses, workshops, seminars, conferences and support (both formal and informal) from initial teacher education colleagues were all identified as suitable strategies to address these learning needs.

School-based teacher educators' professional learning

As we saw in the last chapter, the term teacher educator is used in this book as an inclusive term to encompass all who are professionally engaged in the initial and ongoing education of teachers, including those who work in universities, colleges and schools. In recent years increasing attention is being paid to the international shift towards more school-based teacher education models (Boyd and Tibke, 2012; Lunenberg, Dengerink and Korthagen, 2014; White, Dickerson and Weston, 2015). In England, these models have, as we saw in Chapter 1, included school-centred initial teacher training schemes (SCITTs), employment-based routes (EBITTs), School Direct, Teach First and the emergence of teaching schools. Such models mean that many teacher educators working in schools find themselves increasingly responsible for organising all aspects of Initial Teacher Training (ITT) including the recruitment of trainees; the design, implementation and evaluation of course components and their assessment (Czerniawski, Guberman and MacPhail, 2017; McNamara, Murray and Phillips, 2017). White, Dickerson and Weston (2015, p 443) divide school-based teacher educator roles into three areas: (i) those associated with a traditional mentoring role, (ii) those associated with a supervisory role across a school or schools and (iii) those associated more commonly with institute-based teacher educators (IBTEs). Teacher educators working in schools are also increasingly responsible for the continuing professional development of qualified school teaching staff within their own institutions.

Evidence of professional learning opportunities for school-based teacher educators (specifically related to their role as teacher educators) is, as yet, limited. A point emphasised by O'Dwyer and Atli (2015, p 6) is that

the lack of focus of in-service educators may represent an important omission given the current importance attached to teachers as life-long learners as a result of endemic professional change.

The presumption that if you can teach young people in schools, you can therefore teach adults how to teach, and how to teach more effectively, has permeated teacher education systems in England since the introduction of the state system towards the end of the nineteenth century. This is perhaps one explanatory factor for why very few formal professional learning opportunities have existed for school-based teacher educators in the past. And yet the knowledge, skills, creativity and emotional endeavour required to teach adults varies considerably in content, form, process and technique to that required when teaching children. The dual identity that school-based teacher educators possess (as both teachers and teacher educators) adds additional complexity in understanding what sorts of professional learning activities are of most value to the profession as a whole.

However, while the literature on school-based teacher educator professional learning might be limited, it is nevertheless growing. A study of university and school-based teacher educators in the Netherlands (Dengerink, Lunenberg and Kools, 2015) has indicated that the preferences of school-based teacher educators vary over time. Teacher educators with less experience were interested in coaching skills, pedagogical content knowledge, their own role within wider communities of teacher educators and opportunities to contribute to the knowledge development of the profession as a whole. They valued participation in seminars, conferences and formal courses and desired greater opportunities for more structured learning arrangements (eg supervision, peer-coaching, etc). However, school-based teacher educators with more than seven years of experience were interested in learning about the policy context of school–university partnerships, curriculum issues at the programme level and the pedagogy of teacher education. These more experienced educators tended to place greater value on professional reading, participating in research projects and the role that experimentation can play within their own professional practice. Common to all groups was the value placed on conversations with colleagues as a significant form of professional learning.

In England, one of the outcomes of governmental policy in initial teacher education since 2010 has been the expanding provision of *professional development* for some teacher educators in some schools, albeit in fragmented and particularised forms. This point has been emphasised by Murray, Lunenberg and Smith (2017):

The emergence of 'Teaching Schools' as recognized centres of excellence, with government funding available to support school-led ITE programmes and school-focused research and development projects, has greatly increased the professional learning opportunities available to school-based educators.

(p 660)

However, in England, opportunities brought about by an expanding school-based system of teacher education might not necessarily result in more effective *professional learning* of its school-based teacher educators. Earley and Bubb (2004) distinguish hard economic utilitarianism, where professional *development* addresses the strategic goals of an institution, from a softer developmental humanism in which professional *learning* caters for valued, confident and motivated staff. There is a danger therefore that in England's marketised and competitive school system, teacher educators working in schools might be subjected to the former rather than the latter.

IN A **NUTSHELL**

When professional development is narrowly and instrumentally conceived as a formal, external activity done to recipients then opportunities for authentic teacher educators' professional learning is limited. If, however, a wider interpretation of professional development is used embracing both formal and informal activities that enable critical professional reflection, then professional development, as a term, has validity. However, I prefer the term professional learning to professional development and define teacher educators' professional learning as both the formal and informal processes that enable them to improve their professional practice throughout their careers with a commitment to transform education for the better. The chapter affirms existing literature that professional learning for teacher educators is deemed far more valuable, not through formal provision and organised programmes, but through informal workplace learning (Boyd, Harris and Murray, 2011; Murray, Lunenberg and Smith, 2017). However, while professional learning opportunities for teacher educators working in schools and universities are on the rise, much more needs to be done to foster the professional learning needs of both groups of educators. One notable difference between these groups centres around the degree of support sought for research activities, which has a greater priority for higher education-based teacher educators. The role that research plays in the professional development of teacher educators will be explored more fully in Chapter 5.

REFLECTIONS ON **CRITICAL ISSUES**

- *Reflecting on different models of professional development and learning introduced in this chapter and their appropriateness in both university and school-based settings can be a starting point in discussions with teacher educators as to what forms of professional learning they might value in their careers as teacher educators.*

- *Laudel and Glaser's notion that academics working in universities have three interrelated careers (ie their cognitive, community and organisational careers) can be really helpful when considering what type of professional learning activity might be of most value, to whom and when. As schools increasingly become research active, school-based teacher educators may find these career distinctions increasingly relevant. Understanding the distinction between these three careers is crucial to understanding why it is so difficult to make that transition from a school teacher to a university academic.*

- *The growth of school-based teacher education is not currently accompanied by a commensurate rise in professional developmental opportunities for this group of teacher educators. While this situation may change in the future, the danger is that those opportunities might prioritise the strategic aims of the institution above those of the individual needs of the teacher educator.*

CHAPTER 4 | RETHINKING A KNOWLEDGE BASE FOR TEACHER EDUCATORS

CRITICAL **ISSUES**

- *How does an awareness of different forms of knowledge add to our understanding of teacher educators' professional learning?*
- *To what extent is the concept of a knowledge base for teacher educators achievable or desirable?*
- *How might the existence of a knowledge base for teacher educators be used to inform their professional learning?*

Introduction

Until relatively recently, literature about the knowledge teacher educators need in order to carry out their work effectively was scarce. Much of the literature that did exist drew primarily on work focusing on the knowledge of teachers rather than that of their educators. Understanding what constitutes teacher educators' knowledge is, however, challenging. Competing definitions of this knowledge appear alongside discussions about what might be considered essential, necessary or desirable by teachers, teacher educators and policy-makers. Formalising this knowledge base is also difficult. As seen in earlier chapters, teacher educators are members of a diverse and at times dislocated profession. Nevertheless, it is important to make a claim that, in some way, the knowledge base of teacher educators differs from that of those they educate. Promoting a common understanding of what this knowledge base might look like can open up dialogues with educators working in different contexts with a view to sharing best practice. It can also be used to defend the significance of research and its central positioning as a foundational pillar of teacher education.

In this chapter I introduce you to general discussions about what is meant by knowledge before looking more closely at how some themes within these discussions have been applied to the knowledge of teachers and teacher educators. The chapter discusses recent developments in the construction of the knowledge base for teacher educators, highlighting, in particular, the work of the International Forum for Teacher Educator Development (InFo-TED) in its development.

Knowledge: a contested concept

Questioning what we mean by knowledge, debating its various forms and acknowledging its multiple contestations have dominated the arts, philosophy, theology and education for millennia. Different writers from these disciplines continue to debate their distinctions between knowledge, content, truth, proposition and belief (eg Mannheim, 1993; Kant, 1998; Bauman, 2004). The French philosopher Jean-Francois Lyotard (1997), for example, voices his concerns about the fragmentation of knowledge in what he considers to be a post-modern world. In that world, knowledge ceases to be an end in itself as it becomes repackaged and commodified into new forms compatible with technological and globalised societal change. While these ideas may appear too abstract for some, they are worth reflecting on within the rapidly transforming landscape of teacher education in schools, colleges, federations, academy chains and universities. Consider, for example, the growth in massive open online courses (MOOCs) and their incorporation into teacher education courses. Acknowledging this fragmenting educational landscape and the opportunities, risks and challenges it poses for teacher education justifies an argument for generating a more robust foundational knowledge base for teacher educators in times of rapid transformation.

Two sets of distinctions within the literature about knowledge and teacher education help this process. First, as has been discussed in Chapter 3, is the distinction between knowledge-*for*-practice, knowledge-*in*-practice and knowledge-*of*-practice. The significance of this focus from practitioners on researching their practice is something we will return to in Chapter 6.

Second, a distinction is made between propositional knowledge, ie so-called factual knowledge often associated with truth claims, for example, the different developmental stages children are said to move through; procedural knowledge, ie the knowledge of how to do something, for example, how to write a lesson plan; and personal knowledge, ie autobiographical facts, first-hand experience and so on. Eraut and Hirsh (2007) define personal knowledge as '*what individual persons bring to situations that enable them to think, interact and perform*' (p 6). Hamilton and Pinnegar (2015) argue that these different categories of knowledge are integrated by teacher educators, rather than separated in the enactment of their practice. For example, the know *what* propositional knowledge that educators engage with (eg the distinction between summative, formative and ipsative assessment) is transformed into the know *how* procedural knowledge (such as how best to start a lesson, mark an exam script or arrange a school outing). These forms of knowledge are guided and adapted by the needs and actions of teacher educators' practice, and in turn they inform the ways in which we, as teacher educators, understand and design curricula, pedagogy and assessment as well as the micro-politics of collegiality in the institutions in which we work:

As teacher educators, we recognise that our deepest knowing about educating teachers is embodied, practical, holistic guided, and organised by our commitments, ethics and relationships.

(Hamilton and Pinnegar, 2015, p 60)

Common to both sets of distinctions above is an emphasis on critical reflection and the interrelationship between that reflection and different forms of professional knowledge. This embodied knowing becomes integrated, in situ, within the practical knowledge that teacher educators have accumulated over time and with experience.

Situated knowledge

The role that situated knowledge (Putnam and Borko, 2000) plays in the professional learning of both teachers and teacher educators is considerable. In contrast to the notion of universal knowledge, situated knowledge relies on knowledge construction. Professional knowledge cannot simply be transferred from an expert to a novice. This knowledge is complex and is constructed and consummated through professional practice. Many teacher educators have gained this knowledge through their own classroom experience as teachers, through their own primary and secondary schooling, in the classrooms and lecture halls in which they teach, when supervising their student teachers in schools and colleges and actively through the process of becoming and being a researcher.

And yet the acknowledgement of the importance situated knowledge plays in teacher education needs to be treated with caution. Situated knowledge can become embroiled within a wider debate about the extent to which pre-service teacher education programmes should be concerned with theoretical knowledge, *'leaving the practical, situated knowledge to be acquired later and largely on the job'* (Tatto et al, 2008, p 21). This historic bifurcation between knowledge generated from theory and practice plays out in many educational policy contexts. One example of this is the notion of *craft knowledge*. Craft knowledge is a concept used to refer to knowledge that is embedded in the everyday practice of individual educators (Leinhardt, 1990). Sennett's (2008) use of the term *craftsmanship* captures the complex and sophisticated orchestration required when enacting this type of knowledge:

[In the] higher stages of skill, there is a constant interplay between tacit knowledge and self-conscious awareness, the tacit knowledge serving as an anchor, the explicit awareness serving as critique and corrective. Craft quality emerges from this higher stage, in judgments made on tacit habits and suppositions.

(Sennett, 2008, p 50)

However, within the English educational context teaching-as-craft is portrayed by policy-makers as an atheoretical act of apprentice-style learning rather than a highly professional orientation informed by both theory and research (Kidd, 2016). This particular interpretation of craft has been deployed by the coalition government in the UK as part of a wider ideological attack on the role that universities play in the development of the teaching profession (Gove, 2010).

Pedagogical content knowledge

Lee Shulman's (1987) work on teachers has been hugely influential in examining teacher educators' knowledge. Writing about teachers, Shulman argued that if teacher knowledge were to be organised into a handbook, then minimally these categories might include:

1. *content knowledge;*
2. *general pedagogical knowledge, with special reference to broad principles and strategies of classroom management and organisation that appear to transcend subject matter;*

3. *curriculum knowledge, with particular grasp of the materials and programmes that serve as 'tools of the trade' for teachers;*

4. *pedagogical content knowledge, an amalgam of content and pedagogy that is uniquely the province of teachers, their own special form of professional understanding;*

5. *knowledge of learners and their characteristics;*

6. *knowledge of educational contexts, ranging from the workings of the group or classroom, the governance and financing of school districts, to the character of communities and cultures; and*

7. *knowledge of educational ends, purposes and values, and their philosophical and historical grounds.*

(Shulman, 1987, p 8)

Of these categories, Shulman's concept of pedagogical content knowledge (PCK) is arguably his most significant contribution to teacher educators. Shulman (1987) argues that it is knowledge of PCK that separates teachers of subject matter from other subject experts (Van Driel and Berry, 2017). PCK comprises two ingredients. The first is the knowledge teachers require to represent specific subject matter (through appropriate examples, visual images, explanations, etc). The second is knowledge of students' learning sufficient to be able to identify their understanding and/or misunderstanding of that subject matter (Shulman, 1987; Van Driel and Berry, 2017). Shulman argues that this knowledge is

not to be construed as 'something' that teachers had in their heads but was a more dynamic construct that described the processes that teachers employed when confronted with the challenge of teaching particular subjects to particular learners in specific settings.

(Shulman, 2015, p 24)

Building on Shulman's ideas, Carlson et al (2015) define PCK as *'the knowledge of, reasoning behind, and enactment of the teaching of particular topics in a particular way with particular students for particular reasons for enhancing student outcomes'* (Carlson et al, 2015, p 24). These discussions about knowledge emphasise the dynamic interrelationship and interdependency of professional knowledge, critical reflection and individuality.

In what they argue is a vision of professional practice for teachers (including their educators), Darling-Hammond and Bransford (2005) have identified three areas of knowledge, skills and dispositions as critical for any teacher to acquire:

1. knowledge of learners and how they learn and develop within social contexts;

2. conceptions of curriculum content and goals: an understanding of the subject matter and skills to be taught in light of the social purposes of education;

3. an understanding of teaching in light of the content and learners to be taught, as informed by assessment and supported by classroom environments.

This framework, the authors argue, provides a set of lenses on any teaching situation that educators can use to reflect on and improve their practice (Darling-Hammond and Bransford, 2005, p 10).

The development of a new knowledge base for teacher educators

As we have seen so far, since the 1980s there has been no shortage of published work exploring and promoting a knowledge base for teachers. However, it is only more recently that attempts have been made to create a knowledge base for teacher educators. Lunenberg, Dengerink and Korthagen (2014) define a knowledge base for teacher educators as

a structured and easily accessible collection of knowledge of the professional community. It includes theoretical, pedagogical and practical knowledge, and offers teacher educators the opportunity to confirm, interconnect, share and further develop their professional knowledge, vision, motivation and practices.

(Lunenberg, Dengerink and Korthagan, 2014, p 6)

Several attempts at identifying and championing such a knowledge base have taken place in recent years. For example, Davey (2013) distinguishes three forms of propositional knowledge for both student teachers and teacher educators: comprehensive subject knowledge and PCK; extensive knowledge of educational theory; and an understanding of schooling and the teaching professional within its national context. Goodwin and Kosnik (2013) have identified five knowledge domains that novice teacher educators and teachers should embrace when critically reflecting on their work:

1. *personal knowledge – autobiography and philosophy of teaching;*
2. *contextual knowledge – understanding of learners, schools and society;*
3. *pedagogical knowledge – content, theories, teaching methods, and curriculum development;*
4. *sociological knowledge – diversity, cultural relevance and social justice;*
5. *social knowledge – cooperative, democratic group process, and conflict resolution.*

(Goodwin and Kosnik, 2013, p 338)

The Dutch Association for Teacher Educators (VELON) has devised its knowledge base made up of four core domains, two specific domains and four extended domains applicable to all teacher educators. The four core domains include:

1. the identity of teacher educators;
2. the pedagogy of teacher education;
3. knowledge about learning and learners;
4. knowledge about teaching and coaching.

The contents of the two specific domains are specific to different groups of teacher educators depending on the type of institution they are working in (eg primary or secondary), and the specific school subject they are specialising in. The four extended domains have been designed with more experienced teacher educators in mind and include:

- *the policy context and participation in networks;*
- *participation and leadership within an institution;*
- *knowledge needed in relation to curriculum and assessment development;*
- *knowledge in relation to carrying out research.*

(Dengerink, 2016, p 45)

Attempts at defining a knowledge base for teacher educators can also take the form of professional standards. In the United States, for example, nine standards have been developed by the Association of Teacher Educators (ATE) to identify accomplished teacher educators. These include modelling, cultural competence, scholarship, professional development, programme development, collaboration, public advocacy, contributing to improving the teacher education profession, and vision (embracing technology, systemic thinking and worldviews about teaching) (ATE, 2017).

These frameworks provide, in different ways, a set of lenses on any teaching situation that teacher educators can use to critically reflect and hopefully improve their practice. However, what these approaches have not attempted to do is provide a common language with which to describe, communicate and discuss the diversity in pan-European teacher education and the implications such diversity has for the professional learning of teacher educators. As we shall see in the next part of this chapter an attempt along these lines is currently underway.

The International Forum for Teacher Educator Development (InFo-TED)

A pan-European initiative to develop a knowledge base for teacher educators has been created by the International Forum for Teacher Educator Development (InFo-TED). This forum comprises leading international teacher educators with representatives from Belgium, Ireland, Israel, the Netherlands, Norway, the UK, Australia and the United States working to promote the professional development of teacher educators. The forum has created and published a conceptual model that underpins this knowledge base (Conway et al, 2015; InFo-TED, 2015; Vanassche et al, 2015). See Figure 4.1.

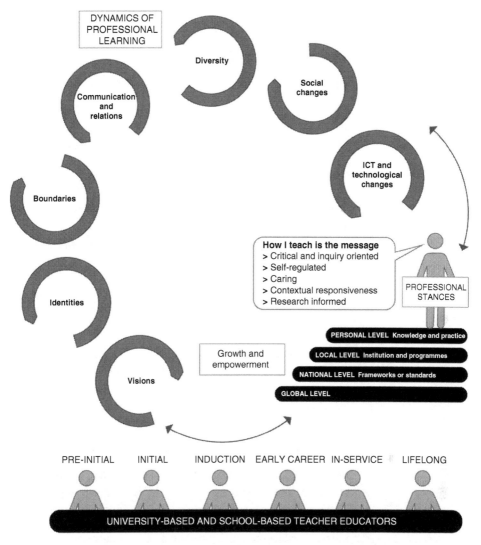

Figure 4.1 Conceptual model for teacher educators' professional development.

A full explanation of this model can be found on the forum's website (http://info-ted.eu/ conceptual-model/), but the diagram here provides a visual link between the conceptual model and the 13 building blocks below. As the model indicates, teacher educators' practices are situated at personal, local, national and global levels of analysis and influence the teacher educator's professional stance. Professional learning is conceived as a constantly dynamic process of lifelong learning and applicable, in different ways, to both university- and school-based teacher educators. Drawing on the development of dynamics of professional learning contained within this conceptual model, InFo-TED has identified a knowledge base for teacher educators consisting of 13 'building blocks' (Table 4.1).

Table 4.1 InFo-TED knowledge base building blocks for teacher educators

1. ICT and technological change	Teacher educators need to engage with ICT and technology when modelling best practices, requiring them to have professional digital competence.
2. Social change	As public intellectuals, teacher educators must embrace knowledge of the changing world in which they prepare teachers while recognising the significance and impact of their practice in that changing world.
3. Diversity	To ensure that the diversity that accompanies social change is fully embraced requires a profession that can critically examine its own ethics, beliefs and practices to ensure that its pedagogy, curriculum and assessment are just, equitable and diverse.
4. Communication and relations	Excellent communication with teacher educators, teachers, policy-makers, administrators and others is crucial for the successful and sustainable professional development of student teachers, teachers and teacher educators.
5. Boundaries	Teacher educators are often operating within different contexts at the same time, eg within professional networks; disciplinary domains; institutional roles; and the physical, social and cultural differences associated with different types of institution. The ability to recognise and successfully navigate the boundaries of these contexts is a marker of an experienced teacher educator.
6. Identities	Professional identities are central to understanding the world of teacher education and the ways in which teacher educators enact their beliefs, values and principles through their work.
7. Visions	Personal, institutional and national visions for teacher education do not always comfortably align. Fostering awareness of these contradictions and contestations can enable teacher educators to become more critically informed, motivated and effective professionals.
8. How I teach is the message	It was Tom Russell (1997) who argued that 'how I teach is the message' should become a keystone in the pedagogy of teacher education. That message must be inquiry oriented, self-regulated, contextually responsive and research informed (Vanassche et al, 2015). It must convey that, as professional learners, teacher educators need to constantly and critically

	reflect on both the formal and informal processes that will enable them to improve their own professional practice throughout their careers with a commitment to transform education for the better.
9. Personal to global – levels of consideration	Professional learning is informed by the professional values of the learner, their institutional context and those related to teacher education policy contexts at the national and international level. Teacher educator attributes are therefore shaped by many, often competing, influences. Understanding how these influences impact on belief and practice is important in informing teacher educators' professional learning.
10. Stages of professional development	Most teacher educators entering the profession receive little or no formal preparation for their roles. The different backgrounds and contexts of teacher educators require tailored pathways for professional learning that recognise their induction, early, mid and senior career professional needs.
11. University-based and school-based teacher educators	Those involved in the provision of professional development of teacher educators must recognise the diversity of their needs. Context matters in the design of such professional development provision and the voices of experienced and novice teacher educators working in university-based or school-based teacher education programmes must inform the nature of professional learning programmes provided.
12. Research	To improve individual practice and knowledge of teacher education as well as contribute to its broader knowledge base, all teacher educators should be involved in research (in one or more of its many forms) as part of a wider commitment to professional development.
13. Assessment	The preparation of future teachers to become assessors of pupil learning is a significant function of assessment in teacher education (Smith, 2016). But the functions of assessment are multiple, complex and highly contextualised and also include the assessment of who can and who cannot become a teacher. The formative, summative and ipsative assessment strategies that teacher educators use and model with their own student/trainee teachers are therefore ones that need carefully constructed professional development.

IN A **NUTSHELL**

The pan-European initiative from InFo-TED to develop a knowledge base for teacher educators is the latest in a series of attempts to promote a common understanding about what kind of knowledge teacher educators need when working in very diverse contexts. In this chapter I have highlighted a variety of interpretations as to what that knowledge might look like, its utility and some of the implications for policy and practice when privileging one form of knowledge over another. The knowledge content of teacher education must be reduced simply to the reproduction of certain sets of actions that any teacher can be trained to perform. Such a reduction risks producing a future generation of teacher educators who focus on the reproduction of techniques, artfully displayed like mannequins, versed only in their experiential knowledge and popularised versions of academic educational theory. Rather, teacher educators must be able to draw on a wider knowledge base that comprises the principles, ideas, theories and practices (Hamilton and Pinnegar, 2015) that enable emerging teachers to become critically reflective, caring and transformative professionals.

REFLECTIONS ON **CRITICAL ISSUES**

This chapter has identified a need for a robust foundational knowledge base for teacher educators at a time of rapid societal change. The fragmenting educational landscape described earlier is one that risks fostering the reconstruction and propagation of teacher education into teacher training and with it the potential de-intellectualisation and reduced criticality of teacher education. This risk alone is a justification enough for the creation of a widely recognised knowledge base for teacher educators and one that caters for the emotion, morality, care, criticality and cultural sensitivity that most educators believe is both central and crucial to their work.

CHAPTER 5 | DOING TEACHER EDUCATION DIFFERENTLY: INTERNATIONAL INITIATIVES

CRITICAL **ISSUES**

- *As a teacher educator, to what extent is it useful to understand teacher education initiatives in different countries?*
- *How do the five turns in education policy (Cochran-Smith, 2016) strengthen our understanding of teacher education in general?*
- *How do the initiatives described in this chapter engage with the artificial binaries of theory and practice in teacher education?*

Introduction

The ability to compare, contrast and understand professional experience in different locations is, I believe, vitally important for well-informed, critically reflective practice. This belief is echoed in one of the largest international studies carried out on teacher educators' professional learning. A pan-European study of 1158 teacher educators from Belgium, England, Ireland, Israel, the Netherlands, Norway and Scotland has indicated a strong desire by teacher educators to be exposed to alternative ways to educate teachers, to learn about developments, both national and international, in teacher education policy and to contribute to teacher education research literature (Czerniawski et al, 2017). But interpreting and applying the work that teacher educators do in one context to that of another can be challenging. Globally, education is in a state of chronic flux with policy-makers constantly re-examining their education systems and how to improve children's performance in schools (European Commission, 2015). Different regional and localised understandings exist about how to educate teachers, the nature of what it means to be a professional teacher educator and what is meant by teaching quality (Gewirtz et al, 2009; Darling-Hammond and Lieberman, 2012). But even within national borders, differences in the configurations of influence and patterns of professional relationships ensure that the experience of being a teacher educator differs considerably for different individuals even within broadly similar contexts and settings. In reference to teacher education, Cochran-Smith (2016) encapsulates this complexity:

Nuanced variations in the historical, socioeconomic, cultural, linguistic, institutional and geopolitical characteristics of particular nations interact with one another and with larger social forces to mediate even those policies that appear on the surface to be very much the same.

(Cochran-Smith, 2016, p x)

This chapter contributes to the book as a whole by offering a degree of insight into some of the more well-documented initiatives taking place in teacher education in different parts of the world. The chapter introduces five turns that Marilyn Cochran-Smith (2016) has identified as characteristic changes affecting teacher education in general. The chapter explores a variety of teacher education initiatives taking place in different countries, ranging from those that focus on the development of teacher educators to those that look at distance learning courses in teacher education. In writing this chapter I am indebted to colleagues who have provided invaluable information about initiatives in which they are involved. These colleagues have been acknowledged at the start of the book.

Five turns in teacher education policy

Significant cultural and epistemic change over the last 30 years, embracing science, technology, the economy, the nature of employment and civil society have inevitably led to changes within both formal and informal education. We have seen throughout this book that the policy gaze on teacher quality, resulting from many of these changes, has led to significant shifts in how teacher education is conceptualised, designed and delivered (McMahon, Forde and Dickson, 2015). In an attempt to understand these shifts Cochran-Smith (2016) identifies five turns in teacher education policy worthy of mention when considering international developments within this field.

1. *The policy turn*: Cochran-Smith argues that in many countries this policy turn *'reflects the shift to a global and competitive knowledge society which has also been a shift to neoliberal economics'* (ibid, p xii). This shift has drawn attention to the quality of education systems and in particular teacher education providers and teachers.

2. *The accountability turn*: Teacher quality is increasingly being associated with standards and outcomes-based educational accountability. This accountability takes into consideration the combination of knowledge, skills and dispositions associated with being a professional teacher. However, the emphasis given to these factors and their importance in terms of how professionalism varies depends on the values orientation within different educational systems.

3. *The practice turn*: At a time when many college and university-based teacher education systems are being challenged in terms of their efficacy, economic value and theoretical contribution, the practice turn is seen as a response to the long-perceived gap between theory and practice. Sometimes referred to as the practicum or practical turn, this phenomenon is powerfully exemplified within the English teacher education system – a system that has in recent years seen a number of governmental reforms prioritising school-led teacher training above the already long-standing university-school partnership system.

4. *The university research turn*: While aspects of the practice turn described above are epitomised within both the English and American teacher education

systems, other education systems in Europe and elsewhere have witnessed the strengthening and consolidation of higher education within initial teacher education. This consolidation can take different forms including efforts to relocate all initial teacher education in universities, the merging or amalgamation of teacher colleges with universities, extending the length of undergraduate and/or graduate degrees and the strengthening role of research in and on initial teacher education.

5. *The equity turn*: Predicated on the belief that many existing arrangements for teacher education do not ensure both excellence and equity for all school students (OECD, 2005; Donlevy, Meierkord and Rajania, 2016), the equity turn focuses on social and educational equity as an achievable goal of education reform.

In very different ways, these five turns offer lenses through which to view and critically reflect on how teacher education is instantiated in different geographical locations. However, these five turns also need to be considered within the context of an historic and contested bifurcation between knowledge generated from theory and knowledge generated from practice. Gordon and O'Brien (2007) note that one of the most common questions student teachers ask is to what extent they can apply the theories they learn in universities to the problems they encounter in the classroom. This question presents a false dichotomy between theory and practice and one that Lewin identified saying that there '*is nothing so practical as good theory*' (Lewin, 1951, p 169). While educational theories are the products of the particular historical and social contexts in which they are generated, they can also be viewed as invaluable '*guides to thought and instruments of interpretation*' (Gordon and O'Brien, 2007, p xiii) that all teachers and teacher educators can use to critically evaluate their own practice. The initiatives described below attempt to bridge the damaging unbridgeable gap between theory and practice in teacher education.

Initiatives in teacher education from around the world

Teaching Academies of Professional Practice (TAPP) – Australia

TAPP is an initiative by the Victorian Department of Education and Training. In 2015, 12 Teaching Academies of Professional Practice were established to improve initial teacher education. Teaching Academies adopt a partnership model to deliver innovative and effective initial teacher education, with a particular focus on the practicum. The initiative aims are to improve teacher preparation and professional learning in schools by building stronger partnerships between schools and universities. The objectives are to:

» improve initial teacher education and the capacity of pre-service teachers to enter the profession;

» immerse pre-service teachers in school environments;

» increase the capacity of schools to provide effective practicum to pre-service teachers;

» strengthen the professional development of current teachers through stronger school-university partnerships;

» influence university course design and delivery of pre-service education by working closely with pre-service education providers;

» provide targeted mentor professional development opportunities for existing teaching staff;

» establish research partnerships to increase the knowledge base about effective initial teacher education.

While this is a government-initiated and funded programme (Victoria State Government, 2017), each TAPP was given the responsibility to develop a programme that meets the needs of its own schools, universities and pre-service teachers. There is also an expectation that research is undertaken, and that sustainable practices are developed and implemented to ensure that the benefits derived from involvement in the TAPP can be continued and built upon in the future. In exploring how this initiative contributed to the professional learning of teacher educators, the Monash Casey TAPP, in the southeastern suburbs of Melbourne, included a research component that explored the professional learning of pre-service teachers, mentor teachers in schools and university-based teacher educators. The findings (Forgasz et al, 2017) about the professional learning of teacher educators suggest:

» increased recognition of the importance of working collaboratively with school-based mentor teachers, and to be seen as equal partners in the education of pre-service teachers;

» the need for time and space to enable schools and universities to work together to develop innovative and effective professional experience programmes. Involvement in the practicum is diminishing for many academic staff, and making the time to develop these programmes outside their normal workload is a huge challenge;

» a reconnection with the realities of school, which for many academics diminish over time, especially when direct involvement in the practicum becomes more limited.

This project represents an attempt to connect university-based and school-based professional learning to begin to better integrate the university curriculum and professional experience in schools (Forgasz et al, 2017).

The Dutch Association for Teacher Educators (VELON)

The Dutch Association for Teacher Educators (VELON) is a professional association of teacher educators in the Netherlands. VELON is independent from schools, universities and colleges and their institutional interests, and membership includes those involved in all aspects of pre-service and in-service teacher education (including those working in schools, colleges and universities). The professional learning of teacher educators is supported through the following activities:

> » *The maintenance of professional standards and a professional register.* Teacher educators can apply to be included in the professional register by passing a self-chosen professional development process and peer-assessment.

> » *Access to a quarterly journal focusing on the interaction between theory and practice in teacher education.* The journal is published jointly with the Flemish Association for Teacher Educators (VELOV).

> » Annual conferences for its members are held. Provision of special interest groups focusing on inclusive education, professional development focusing on research activities, workplace learning and information technology is provided.

The organisation has been responsible for the production of a knowledge base for teacher education (see Chapter 4) first published in 2011. In the Netherlands more than 80 per cent of student teachers are educated at colleges, which traditionally have not included research tasks as part of their assessment strategies. Over the last decade, however, these colleges have started to acknowledge the importance of student teacher engagement in research. Student teachers are now requested to carry out a research project in their final year of their teacher education courses. In turn this has led to greater attention being paid to the research competencies of teacher educators and their professional needs in supporting their own students. *Teacher educators study their own practice* is one project that has emerged as a result of these developments with three cohorts of teacher educators receiving professional support over the course of one year. Findings from studies of this initiative indicate that participation has contributed to the participants' professional learning, improvement in their practice, broadened their perspectives on research and enabled them to better understand the pitfalls student teachers meet in carrying out their own research projects (Lunenberg and Korthagen Zwart, 2010; Berry, Geursen and Lunenberg, 2015).

The Norwegian National Research School in Teacher Education (NAFOL)

Norway has recently experienced considerable structural change in its teacher education provision. These changes have been underpinned by government policies supportive of a research-based teacher education system with student teachers engaging in research and supported by research-competent teacher educators. Since 2004, teachers working in upper secondary school have been educated at universities on five-year integrated teacher education programmes. These programmes integrate a master's qualification in the teaching discipline (eg mathematics, history, English) with a teaching qualification that includes courses in education, subject methodology as well as the practicum.

From 2017 a similar programme within university colleges was introduced for primary school teacher education. Whereas the universities do not need accreditation from the Norwegian Agency for Quality Assurance in Education (NOKUT) to create new master programmes, university colleges do. When the reform was announced, university colleges immediately engaged in planning new teacher education programmes designed to meet NOKUT's requirements for graduate education. However, this move created tensions within the system as a whole as many within the university college sector felt they were not being trusted by policy-makers to offer professional education at master's level despite possessing a lengthy experience of educating teachers. These tensions were exacerbated by the inclusion of criteria for accreditation emphasising the number of professors in the programme and the number of research-competent staff with a doctorate.

This upgrading of teacher education to a master's level should be seen in the light of the international trend towards research-based teacher education that this book has already examined. All education at a graduate level in Norway requires a research dissertation. This means that Norwegian student teachers will require a large number of research-competent teacher educators who can supervise the students' master's dissertations. This can be challenging for university colleges, as many of their teacher educators do not have doctorates, as their main responsibilities lie in teaching rather than research. Recognising these challenges, the Norwegian Research Council, acting on behalf of the Norwegian government has, since 2010, been financing the creation of the Norwegian National Research School in Teacher Education (NAFOL). NAFOL provides courses in supervision, academic writing and methodology, as well as a variety of networks for teacher educators engaging in doctoral studies. The candidates come from all levels of teacher education, from pre-school to upper-secondary school, as well as qualified teachers and has been established to strengthen a research-based perspective in these different levels. NAFOL is organised as a partnership between seven Norwegian universities and 12 university colleges. It is co-ordinated by the Faculty of Social Sciences and Technology Management, at the Norwegian University of Science and Technology (NTNU) in Trondheim, Norway.

Distance Learning Initial Teacher Education – Scotland

The Distance Learning Initial Teacher Education – Professional Graduate Diploma in Education (DLITE PGDE) is a part-time teaching qualification programme provided by the University of Aberdeen, Scotland, and is run in partnership with the local education authority. The qualification is recognised by the General Teaching Council for Scotland (GTCS) and it enables graduates to gain a teaching qualification whilst remaining in their current employment (provided their employer can allow leave of absence to undertake full-time placements in schools). Hailed in a report for the General Teaching Council for Scotland as *'an example of innovative new practice'* (Hartshorn et al, 2005), the DLITE PGDE programme was born out of the first distance learning PGDE programme in Scotland provided by the University of Aberdeen in partnership with Highland Council. Since that original development, the DLITE PGDE model has capitalised on the partnership between the university and the participating local authorities, with each of the partners collaborating to co-construct and support the academic and professional learning of the DLITE participants as a jointly staffed initiative (Bain, Bruce and Weir, 2016). This partnership development resulted in Aberdeenshire Council, one of the local authority partners with the University of Aberdeen, gaining national recognition with the COSLA Excellence award in 2017 for the *'creative approach it has taken to attracting new recruits to the teaching profession'* (Aberdeenshire Council, 2017).

The DLITE PGDE participants are guaranteed placements and an induction year of teaching within the partnership authority, ensuring that local graduates are available as teachers within the local authority. For the local authority participants, involvement in DLITE enables an in-depth insight of the PGDE teaching qualification, creating a greater understanding of the stage of development of the student teachers as they progress through the PGDE initial teacher education (ITE) qualification. It also provides an opportunity for greater cohesion between the ITE phase of development and the induction year. For the university tutors, the partnership brings close links with the local authority and an opportunity to further shape the PGDE learning and enhance professional learning for the school-based mentors. This bringing together of the different professional communities, across different local authorities and the university tutoring teams, enables new ways of supporting professional learning of teachers to develop, with each of the partners gaining from the bridging of different communities of practice.

The International Forum for Teacher Educator Development (InFo-TED)

In 2012 InFo-TED, an international group of leading teacher educators, came together to discuss and support the professional learning needs of teacher educators and to exchange best research, policy and practice (Vanassche et al, 2015). The forum comprises representatives from Australia, Belgium, England, Ireland, Israel, the Netherlands, Norway, Scotland and the USA. Specifically, the forum aims to:

» develop and implement a knowledge base for teacher educators – addressing the diverse tasks and roles teacher educators fulfil in diverse educational contexts;

» translate the knowledge base into an international professional development programme – bringing together teacher educators from different countries to co-develop and evaluate professional development strategies for teacher educators nationally and locally;

» develop and implement guidelines for induction and professional learning programmes – developing web-based principles on how to support teacher educators' collaborative professional learning, taking into account their roles and responsibilities within diverse settings;

» explore how an enduring international supportive structure can be implemented for professional development activities – exploring how the InFo-TED knowledge base (see Chapter 4), the study programme and the guidelines for professional development can be implemented, maintained and further developed.

This forum has generated several publications on the professional learning of teacher educators (see Vanaasche et al, 2015; Lunenberg et al, 2016; Czerniawski, Guberman and MacPhail, 2017; Czerniawski et al 2018; Kelchtermans, Smith and Vanderlinde, 2017; Murray, Lunenberg and Smith, 2017) as well as European Commission (ERASMUS+) funding to develop an international summer academy for teacher educators, which will open in 2018 (InFo-TED website: http://info-ted.eu/forum/).

IN A **NUTSHELL**

Experiential knowledge is knowledge forged within the immediate context of particular experiences. For teachers and teacher educators, this is valuable in its own right, but learning from context alone is a process that is inherently conservative. It evades the benefits gained from looking outward to alternative professional action or inward through the lenses of theory and research-informed practice. Earlier in this chapter I referred to the historic bifurcation between theory and practice in initial teacher education (ITE). Current understandings of initial teacher education often construct conceptual binaries around practice and theory, universities and schools (Murray and Mutton, 2016). The initiatives that this chapter has introduced you to are those that have attempted, in different ways, to confront, grapple and eradicate these artificial binaries. In valuing and celebrating partnerships between universities and schools they have, in different ways, encountered the policy turns that Cochran-Smith (2016) has written about and which are briefly summarised in this chapter. The internationalisation of school-based teacher education poses genuine questions around the future of university-based teacher education, the educational research that underpins it and the dominant conceptualisations of professional learning models in years to come (Czerniawski and Ulvik, 2014). But there is much to learn from the initiatives described in this chapter – initiatives that are underpinned by different values, different discourses and different trajectories that nuance the ways in which these policy turns are enacted.

REFLECTIONS ON **CRITICAL ISSUES**

To what extent can we draw useful knowledge from teacher education initiatives in different parts of the word? Comparisons carry with them risks. Oversimplified findings and superficial conclusions often accompany an inability to grasp complexities in language, history and culture. Alexander (2005) notes that '*the language of education contains few universals and educational conversation across cultures is laced with pitfalls for the unwary*'

(Alexander, 2005, p 5). Different historical starting points of education systems combined with differences in institutional structures also make meaningful generalisation, at best, problematic. But there is much to learn from, as well as in, countries where the professional learning of teacher educators is strongly supported and critical, research-informed practice is encouraged, nurtured and celebrated. In increasingly globalised times, national educational debates about teacher education need international perspectives. Teacher educators, working in increasingly beleaguered higher education institutions, especially in England, need to be able to draw not just on the knowledge and best practice generated in different communities of practice but the enthusiasm, hope, creativity and wisdom that characterises this heterogeneous occupational group.

CRITICAL **ISSUES**

- *To what extent is it important that teacher educators become teacher educator researchers?*
- *What distinction exists between consumers and producers of research and why might that distinction be useful?*
- *What professional learning needs are specific to the teacher educator researcher?*

Introduction

The use of evidence, enquiry and evaluation lie at the very heart of what it means to be both a teacher and teacher educator. Engaging in research not only contributes to the professional development of teacher educators, but to the body of knowledge of the profession and to teaching and learning in general (Loughran, 2014; Willemse and Boei, 2017). This point is powerfully made in the foreword to the BERA-RSA Inquiry into Research and Teacher Education:

Research and enquiry has a major contribution to make to effective teacher education in a whole variety of different ways; it also contributes to the quality of students' learning in the classroom and beyond. Teachers and students thrive in the kind of settings that we describe as research-rich, *and research-rich schools and colleges are those that are likely to have the greatest capacity for self-evaluation and self-improvement.*

(BERA-RSA, 2014, p 3)

However, depending on their trajectory into the profession, many teacher educators find themselves ill-equipped to carry out research. Those who do engage in research can often find themselves confronting institutional values in universities that grant greater symbolic intellectual capital to abstract theorising and/or more positivist research outputs than to the more qualitative, exploratory forms of research that typify much research activity in education. It is also worth remembering that, in contrast to the physical and natural sciences, researchers in education very often work on their own. This relative isolation can exacerbate an already challenging employment context where many teacher educators juggle the competing demands of teaching, administration, marketing, bidding and research. In this chapter I will therefore explore some of the challenges teacher educators face in becoming teacher educator researchers and will discuss the relationship between research-based knowledge and scholarship and how both can inform the professional learning and practice of teacher educators.

Teacher educators as teacher educator researchers

A growing body of literature has argued the importance of teacher educators as researchers (BERA-RSA, 2014; Loughran, 2014; Kelchtermans, Smith and Vanderlinde, 2017). The Organisation for Economic Cooperation and Development (OECD) defines researchers as

professionals engaged in the conception or creation of new knowledge. They conduct research and improve or develop concepts, theories, models, techniques instrumentation, software or operational methods.

(OECD, 2015)

But what exactly do we mean by research? Fully cognisant of the breadth, depth and diversity of educational research and the diversity of those who engage in research activity, the BERA-RSA Inquiry has taken a deliberately inclusive and wide-ranging definition of research. By research, the report's authors mean any deliberate investigation that is carried out with a view to learning more about a particular educational issue (BERA-RSA, 2014, p 42). As teacher educators, many of us engage with research in one way or another, formally and/or informally, when we plan and prepare our teaching, presentations, reports and publications. The reading we do includes almost any form of publication that is research informed (eg journal articles, textbooks, blogs, policy documentation). One can identify this preparatory scholarly activity as research, albeit research with a small *r* (Murray, Czerniawski and Barber, 2014). Akin to Boyer's (1990) notion of the scholarship of teaching, this type of research can take the form of reading to inform (and hopefully enhance) personal and professional practice. However, Cochran-Smith (2005) argues that as smart consumers of research teacher educators need to do more than just critically read and understand the epistemological background of research articles and reports. In addition to this scholarly disposition they need also to be capable of conducting research into their own practices and programmes

taking our own professional work as educators as a research site and learning by systematically investigating our own practice and interpretive frameworks in ways that are critical, rigorous, and intended to generate both local knowledge and knowledge that is useful in more public spheres.

(Cochran-Smith, 2005, p 220)

Far from just being research consumers, teacher educators can generate new forms of knowledge – research with a capital *R*. This form of research engagement and knowledge production has been inherently linked to the improvement of teacher educators' own practice and the development of a public knowledge base for teacher education (Loughran, 2014; Tack and Vanderlinde, 2014). Mindful of the significance Cochran-Smith (2003) pays to the social, historical, cultural and political context in which professional practice is situated, research of this nature can improve daily practice through systematic and critical inquiry. But for this to happen, teacher educators need to develop what Tack and Vanderlinde (2016) term as *'researcherly disposition'* (ibid, p 4). This disposition, they argue, consists of three interrelated dimensions.

1. *An affective dimension*: the extent to which a teacher educator values his or her role as a teacher educator researcher.

2. *A cognitive dimension*: the teacher educator's perceived ability to engage with research as both a consumer and producer of knowledge.

3. *A behavioural dimension*: the teacher educator's tendency to engage in research activities as both a consumer and producer of knowledge.

While these dimensions focus on the indwelling, visceral and psychological factors affecting their choice of action, Willemse and Boei (2017) identify both agentic and structural features that, they argue, influence teacher educators into becoming researchers.

» *Teacher educators' views of the role as researcher*: many teacher educators may prioritise what they see as their primary role (ie teacher of teachers) – above that of carrying out research. Different academic disciplines (eg history, physics and sociology) may also be associated with different methodological approaches and this might affect the extent to which some teacher educators feel they possess sufficient methodological expertise to engage in research activity.

» *The practical challenges of the role of researcher*: the availability of sufficient resources to enable research engagement (time, money, equipment, etc); and the extent to which staff evaluation mechanisms value research (in contrast to teaching performativity and other roles associated with their job specification).

» *The existence of research groups and programmes*: the extent to which dedicated structured support is available to foster teacher educators' professional development in conducting research (including the existence of a clearly defined research culture).

Developing this researcherly *'habit of mind'* (Tack and Vanderlinde, 2014, p 301) can also be challenging depending on the employment context. While schools are increasingly becoming research active, for many school-based teacher educators, finding space and time for research can be a huge ask when they might view their primary role as teaching pupils. For ex-teachers working in university education departments, while their first-order expertise (Murray and Male, 2005) is teaching, they may or may not possess a master's level qualification and therefore any research experience at all. In their transition to becoming second-order practitioners within a university, ie teaching about teaching, these educators can find themselves working alongside university colleagues whose first-order experience is in research, not teaching, ie working with colleagues with disciplinary expertise outside the field of education, eg in sociology and psychology (Smith, 2015). In all cases these challenges should have significant implications for the commitment institutional senior leadership teams give to dedicated professional development provision targeting the research (and teaching) potential of all their staff.

Moving closer to a research-rich environment in teacher education

When educational research within the UK comes under the gaze of critical others (eg academics from other disciplines, practitioners, policy-makers, parents and senior leadership teams) our discipline holds up well. Results from the UK's 2014 Research Excellence Framework (the system for assessing the quality of research in British higher education systems) concluded in its report that

> » *92 per cent of activity was judged to be of international standard (2* or above);*
>
> » *66 per cent was judged to be internationally excellent or better (3* or above);*
>
> » *and 30 per cent was judged to be world-leading (4*).*

(REF, 2015, p 103)

The report went on to confirm *'that considerable improvement in research quality in education has taken place compared with 2008, and that a significant proportion of the submitted educational research is world-leading'* (ibid, 103). That said, it is also the case that while the relationship between research and teacher education is celebrated in many countries (eg Finland, Singapore and Norway), the contribution of both research and higher education to Initial Teacher Education (ITE) in England has been marginalised in recent years, particularly for those working in teaching-intensive universities (Menter, 2015; Willemse and Boei, 2017). The transformation of teacher education to a more marketised, and seemingly demand-led system (Gewirtz, 2013), has paved the way for the recruitment and training of student teachers to be placed in the hands of schools, federations of schools, academy chains, teaching schools and teaching school alliances. Ensuring that universities are pivotal to research-informed provision is difficult within England's school-led teacher education system – a system increasingly taking on roles in initial teacher education, continuing professional development and research (Murray and Mutton, 2016). Reduced funding to universities as a result of governmental austerity measures has exacerbated this *'(re)turn to the practical'* (Furlong and Lawn, 2010, p 6), leaving many university senior leadership teams in teaching-intensive universities prioritising undergraduate courses for their income, above many post-graduate courses including those devoted to teacher education. This diminution of the role that research plays in teacher education is not helped by the fact that the current teaching standards in England make no mention of research (DfE, 2013). Taken together these structural changes have limited the potential for many teacher educators to contribute strongly and consistently to research-informed teacher education programmes including those that purport to offer master's level accreditation (McNamara and Murray, 2013).

Mindful of the sweeping nature and pace of these structural changes and the impact they might have on the educational research environment, the BERA-RSA Inquiry (2014) report considered how research contributes to the development of professional practice, school practice and the outcomes for learners of all ages and abilities. The report identified four main ways in which research can make a contribution to teacher education.

1. *The content of teacher education programmes may be informed by research-based knowledge and scholarship, emanating from a range of academic disciplines and epistemological traditions.*

2. *Research can be used to inform the design and structure of teacher education programmes.*

3. *Teachers and teacher educators can be equipped to engage with and be discerning consumers of research.*

4. *Teachers and teacher educators may be equipped to conduct their own research, individually and collectively, to investigate the impact of particular interventions or to explore the positive and negative effects of educational practice.*

(BERA-RSA, 2014, p 5)

The authors of the BERA-RSA Inquiry use the term 'research-rich' to refer to environments in which research thrives (BERA-RSA, 2014). At the beginning of the report it states that:

The Inquiry makes the case for the development, across the UK, of self-improving education systems in which all teachers become research literate and many have frequent opportunities for engagement in research and enquiry. This requires that schools and colleges become research-rich environments in which to work. It also requires that teacher researchers and the wider research community work in partnership, rather than in separate and sometimes competing universes. Finally, it demands an end to the false dichotomy between HE and school-based approaches to initial teacher education.

(BERA-RSA, 2014, p 1)

The report advocates 10 principles for a research-rich, self-improving education system.

The 10 principles of self-improving and research-rich education systems

1. Teachers share a common responsibility for the continuous development of their research literacy.

2. During the course of qualifying and throughout their careers, teachers have multiple opportunities to engage in research and enquiry, collaborating with colleagues in other schools and colleges and with members of the wider research community.

---

3. Commissioners of education research build teacher engagement into commissioning processes so that wherever possible teachers are active agents in research.

4. Producers of new research knowledge endeavour to make their research findings as freely available, accessible and usable as possible.

5. Research literacy has a prominent place in development programmes such that the development of research-rich school and college environments is seen as a key leadership responsibility.

6. Inspection frameworks explicitly recognise the importance of research literacy to teachers' professional identity and practice.

7. Every learner is entitled to teaching that is informed by the latest relevant research.

8. Every teacher is entitled to work in a research-rich environment that supports the development of their research literacy and offers access to facilities and resources that support sustained engagement with and in research.

9. Policy-makers of all persuasions – and those who seek to influence policy – encourage, and are responsive to, the findings of the educational research, both in policy formulation and in implementation strategies.

10. There is a sustained and growing systemic capacity to support educational research at the level of the individual school or college, through local and regional networks, embedded in teachers' terms and conditions and across the wider research community based in universities and elsewhere.

(Adapted from BERA-RSA, 2014, pp 24–25)

Identifying the professional learning needs of teacher educator researchers

My colleagues and I have written elsewhere (Czerniawski et al, 2018) that the increased national and international rankings pressure on universities has meant greater pressure on university-based academics in teacher education, as they work to acquire a doctorate and publish in peer-reviewed research outlets (Stern, 2016). That said, national audits can also *redefine* what is meant by research, *narrow* the criteria for what counts as research and *who* is acknowledged to be a researcher (Murray, Lunenberg and Smith, 2017). This is, at the time of writing, the case in the UK where the next Research Excellence Framework, widely referred to as the *REF* and scheduled for 2021, has an impact on who is and who is not defined as a researcher by employer institutions. The resurgence of educational science has been accompanied by enthusiasm on the part of many policy-makers for more medicalised educational research methodologies such as randomised control trials (Whitty, 2016). For many teacher educators working in universities, their small-scale, practice-based research is often not compatible with this methodological paradigm nor deemed *REFable* by their institutions. But as a research auditing framework it is also one that gives no consideration at all to research that might be carried out by teachers and teacher educators working in schools.

Addressing the skills gap many teacher educators face when working in universities is a challenge not solely confined to the UK. A recent large-scale pan-European study carried out by the InFo-TED group (Czerniawski et al, 2017) (see also Chapter 4) provided an inter-national and comparative needs analysis through a survey of 1158 higher education-based teacher educators in Belgium, Ireland, Israel, the Netherlands, Norway and the UK. Teacher educators in all countries commented on their need to develop their research skills in the areas of writing, research methodology and methods, research ethics and data analysis. But the study also identified more foundational needs, for example, how to develop an idea into a viable research project, how to write for the *right* journals, locate the best conferences and access the most suitable professional networks. At the time of writing no such similar study has (yet) been carried out addressing the needs of teacher educators working in schools.

While this chapter has highlighted my concerns about the implications of what a school-led education system might mean for the sustainability of a vibrant research culture, it also offers complex hope. The creation of *Research Leads* in some schools in England in recent years has been accompanied by debates over the extent to which all teachers in schools can and should be involved in research, the nature and value of *experiential* and *craft* knowledge and what is meant by *research-informed* teaching (Bennett 2016; McAleavy, 2016). These debates and the emerging spaces in which they occur challenge the val-idity of current research auditing mechanisms such as the *REF*, which does not embrace research activity in schools. They also challenge more conservative conceptions of research capability and capacity that have traditionally embodied more *scientific*/positivist ideals. Acknowledging the value practitioner-based research has in professional learning, Murray (2011) has called for the '*re-framing of the place of research in induction and pro-fessional development in teacher education*'. For policy-orientated logical coherence, this reframing must take place if *school-led*, research-informed teacher education remains the government's objective. This does, however, pose a wicked policy problem (Roberts, 2000) for any government whose research auditing mechanisms only address research outputs from universities. For this reframing to take place, I hope that policy-makers, subject and research associations, teachers and teacher educators in school, colleges and universities can draw on the 10 principles detailed in the BERA-RSA Inquiry. In doing so it is also hoped that what is produced is a healthy education research community that, after Whitty (2016), is one that is a '*broad church, encompassing activity that responds directly to external pri-orities, but also curiosity- or discipline-led inquiry*' (ibid, p 1).

IN A **NUTSHELL**

In this chapter I have explored some of the challenges teacher educators face in becoming teacher educator researchers and discussed the relationship between research-based knowledge, scholarship and how both can inform the professional learning and practice of teacher educators as smart consumers and producers of research. With colleagues I have written elsewhere (Czerniawski et al, 2018) about our fears regarding the potential diminution of the role research plays in the quality of ITE, teacher educators' professional learning and teacher professionalism. Gewirtz (2013) argues that the danger in talking about *research-informed* teacher education is that this reinforces a reductionist, techno-engineering model of teacher education where future teachers, uncritically, simply implement *what works* rather than critically reflect on their practice, its impact and rationale. The nurturing of teacher educators' scholarly and researcherly dispositions is a prerequisite for authentic and enduring professional learning and professional development. It is also a prerequisite for future practice in teacher education that will support a new generation of teachers to go beyond *what works* to engage in a genuine educational transformation of the system and its learners.

REFLECTIONS ON **CRITICAL ISSUES**

- *As part of a self-improving, research-rich education system, bringing together different teacher educators from different types of institution (schools, colleges and universities) is important. This chapter has highlighted the hierarchical divisions between different forms of research (ie practitioner versus large-scale, funded projects) as well as addressing hierarchy in research, teaching and the inseverable relationship between the two.*

- *Whatever the future holds for teacher education in universities and schools, for this to be education (as opposed to simply* training*), student teachers must be encouraged and empowered to research their own practice. For this research to be authentic, effective and transformative, those that empower, champion and nurture that research must be research aware, research literate and research active.*

- *If teacher educators' lack of time and of confidence in their research and writing skills are barriers for teacher educators being teacher educator researchers, then opportunities need to be created to embed research within their day-to-day practice. Acknowledgement of these barriers is important, not least when considering the future supply chain to universities of teacher educators, many of whom, as former schoolteachers, have (in the English context) come from an increasingly school-based, occupational teacher training model rather than a more university-structured ITE programme.*

CHAPTER 7 | CONCLUSION: MOVING ON ... ONE STEP AT A TIME

CRITICAL **ISSUES**

- *In what ways can the issues we have looked at in this book inform your future development as a teacher educator?*
- *To what extent can teacher educators in all employment contexts engage with, and in, research?*
- *How can you use this book to critically reflect on the development of your own professional practice?*

Introduction

As teacher educators in the twenty-first century we are not just *teachers of teachers* (Lunenberg et al, 2017). Depending on where we work, we are often involved in coaching, mentoring, researching, assessing, marketing, bid writing and designing curricula. We are the gatekeepers, hand-holders and emotional carers of a future generation of classroom practitioners. I hope that this book has, in some way, contributed to your understanding of those hybrid, poly-contextualised identities that were discussed in Chapter 2. Understanding the relationship between these identities and different forms of professional learning is important if our profession is to move to one more fully supported by future politicians, policy-makers, teachers and members of the public. At a time of systemic change in the education systems of many countries, it is worth remembering that teachers in schools are increasingly being asked to be responsible for the education and training of future teachers. In Chapter 3 we learnt from McNamara, Murray and Jones (2014) how the historical trajectory England has taken in terms of workplace learning has shifted from the nineteenth-century classroom-based apprenticeship model of teacher education to its current yet qualitatively different descendent. This development is cautiously welcomed while at the same time acknowledging the potential threat it poses to universities, the teaching profession and teacher education in general. This chapter draws together these themes and how they can be used to inform the future professional learning of all teacher educators. A checklist of professional learning activities is included in this chapter as well as a series of critical reflection questions for you to consider in your next steps in this profession.

A note of caution for those championing school-led teacher education

This book has drawn attention to the fact that many teacher educators engage, in varying degrees, with hybridised discourses centred around both practice and theory. While different models of teacher education vary, for many teacher educators this synergy emerges perhaps from our own previous experience as a student teacher within a higher education and school partnership. If McNamara, Murray and Jones (2014) are right in their assertion that England represents an interesting *test-bed* in terms of the trajectory school-led teacher education can take, then these developments need to be watched with caution. Many schools are replacing universities at the heart of the decision-making process in terms of who can/cannot be recruited into the profession. At a time when many countries are increasing their provision of school-based teacher education, colleagues and I have written elsewhere (Czerniawski et al, 2018) that this rapid and radical change might bring with it unforeseen externalities that include the following.

1. The diminution of the role that research plays in informing the quality of initial teacher education and teacher professionalism. Gewirtz (2013) argues that the danger in talking about research-informed teacher education is that rather than critically reflecting and questioning taken-for-granted assumptions, this particular discourse reinforces a reductionist, techno-engineering model of teaching where teachers, uncritically, implement *what works*. These concerns have been picked up in the UK with the BERA-RSA Inquiry into the role of research in teacher education (BERA-RSA, 2014) and the Carter Review (2015).

2. Teachers developing limited and limiting pedagogies as a result of being trained and prepared to teach in *one* school rather than being *educated* to teach in *all* schools. As part of a deregulation agenda the shift in the locus of control of teacher education from universities to schools has the potential to shift '*the focus from pedagogy to content knowledge and verbal expression, maintaining [the belief] that pedagogy and professional learning are best acquired on the job*' (Grimmet and Chinnery, 2009, p 10).

3. The diminution in the authority and availability of university-based teacher educators offering high-quality research-informed advice, guidance and support to student/trainee teachers as they are increasingly involved in relationship maintenance (Ellis et al, 2013). The fear here is that as universities in England become ever more reliant on schools to engage their services, universities and university tutors prioritise partnership arrangements with specific schools and colleges over and above the research and supervision required to ensure the high quality of the practicum in general.

This book has drawn attention to the amazing work carried out by teacher educators working in schools, colleges and universities. However, as a test-bed (McNamara, Murray and Jones, 2014), both the teacher education initiatives, School Direct (SD) and SCITTs, in England represent a significant threat to higher education institutions (HEIs) not just in terms of the decreasing student numbers (and therefore income) but also the extent to which educational research remains viable within the academy. With the rise of school-led teacher education in England this system risks being fuelled by a future generation of twenty-first-century school-based teacher educators, institutionally recruited, developed, situated and positioned within limiting mono-cultural understandings of what teacher education is or indeed should be.

Nurturing communities of enquiry

Unless research is valued for its capacity as a tool of professional learning by all stakeholders in teacher education, we risk the marginalisation and eventual disappearance of a theory-informed future teaching profession. Peiser (2016) reminds us that UK education policy prioritises instrumental knowledge over a wider professional understanding of teacher education and the work of teacher educators. This is significant when considering the issues raised in Chapter 6 regarding the role research plays in the lives of teacher educators. While, in England, the increasing take-up of school-led teacher education poses a threat to research capacity in universities, it nevertheless does offer some degree of hope that practitioner-based research in schools might increase. While reference to research in the English teachers' standards is absent, it is nevertheless embedded as one of the responsibilities of designated teaching schools (NCTL, 2014). However, in the wake of governmental austerity measures in the UK, the teacher education research landscape in schools, colleges and universities risks fragmentation and marginalisation by policy-makers whose ears are more attuned to more positivist research methodology (eg randomised control trials) than other more wide-ranging approaches to research characteristic of the field of teacher education and its educators (eg action research and other forms of small-scale exploratory research).

Chapter 6 drew attention to the BERA-RSA (2014) Inquiry, a report commissioned to ascertain the role research plays in teacher education. The report states that '*schools and colleges become research-rich environments in which to work*' (BERA-RSA, 2014, p 2). The report highlights the significance of *research engagement*, ie the involvement of teachers and educational leaders in carrying out research and *research literacy*, ie that teachers should be

familiar with a range of research methods, with the latest research findings and with the implications of this research for day-to-day practice, and for education policy and practice more broadly.

(BERA-RSA 2014, p 40)

For this to happen we need a profession of teacher educators who are research-literate themselves. After Dewey (1902) and drawing on work from the Netherlands, Willemse and Boei (2017) have created nine design principles they consider important in developing teacher educators' communities of enquiry regardless of whether they work in schools, colleges or universities. These principles embrace all teacher educators but particularly those who may have little or no experience of conducting research or supervising students' research.

Nine design principles for developing communities of enquiry

1. Research should be conducted together in small groups of six to eight educators to ensure mutual collaboration and decision-making.

2. The subject of inquiry is communally chosen and derived from practice.

3. Frequent meetings (eg every four weeks) to take place with the community of enquiry.

4. Fixed dates for meetings that provide a clear exchange of commitment and expectations of the community.

5. Meetings to follow commonly defined stages of research (problem definition, literature search, research question formulation, instrument design, planning and gathering of data, analyses, sharing the results with others).

6. Each meeting has to be organised around three themes: (1) explore existing research and exchanging prior knowledge; (2) work on the research project; (3) reflecting on learning experiences and the relationship between those experiences and supervising pre-service teachers' research.

7. In pairs and between meetings participants should reflect and engage with tasks to guarantee the continuation of the research.

8. Experienced teacher educator researchers should participate as full members and as mentors of the community of enquiry.

9. After collaborative consideration and dialogue the results of the research are shared through dialogue, conference presentation and publications.

(ibid, pp 210–211)

Teacher educators are professional learners

Chapter 3 showed that while professional learning opportunities for teacher educators working in schools and universities are on the rise, much more needs to be done to foster the professional learning needs of both groups of educators. This issue has been recognised in a report from the European Commission (2013, p 22):

As most teacher educators entering the profession have not undertaken specific training, the induction phase is crucial in developing understanding of their particular roles, which entail second-order teaching competences. Research on the experiences of beginning teacher educators shows that the difficult transition from teacher to teacher educator can be challenging, when it comes to developing a clear understanding of their role, building professional confidence, learning the language of the profession, and gaining access to the knowledge base on teacher learning.

The same report identifies professional learning activities for teacher educators that can focus on the following range of content areas, with wide variations depending on their roles (eg within universities or schools):

- *new developments in society and education with a significant impact on teachers and teacher educators – for instance, ICT, second language learning, diversity and inclusion, learning to learn competences;*

- *specific competences in innovation and change management;*

- *courses for school-based teacher educators or mentors concerning the methodology, pedagogy and didactics of teacher education;*

- *programmes engaging teacher educators in practice-based research in both school and university settings – school-based teacher educators, if inexperienced in doing research, may find this useful in helping them meet the expectations of the newly joined higher education community.*

(ibid, p 23)

As teacher educators we must not lose sight of what our primary focus should be – the preparation of future professional teachers who are equipped to develop young people to play their part in the formation of a socially, economically and environmentally just and viable society.

Moving your career forward one step at a time

As this book draws to a close I hope you have found it useful to you as a source of critical reflection on how you can enhance your professional practice and career trajectory. Taking time to reflect on your own professional trajectory feels like a luxury rather than a professional necessity. Finding someone (eg a professional mentor) who you trust and can sit down with to talk about your professional development is essential to moving your own career forward. You might find the following questions useful in preparation for such a conversation.

Reflection points

» What practices have you tended to adopt the most (in teaching, research, networking and writing)?

» To what extent are these practices effective?

» What might you learn from other colleagues and how best can you accommodate their practice into your own?

» Against what measurements or values do you examine your own practice?

» To what extent could you explore alternative values in critically evaluating, as well as celebrating, your own practice?

» What opportunities are there in your own institution for career support and development?

» What opportunities exist within and outside your own institution to address your professional strengths and weaknesses?

» To what extent are you fully aware of the sources of funding available to you to develop your own professional learning?

» What professional networks exist (eg subject associations, trade unions, university networks, learned societies/research associations) that could support your career development?

» To what extent could you benefit from subject and methodological knowledge development?

» To what extent would you find it beneficial to observe or be observed by colleagues in order to improve your own pedagogic practice?

And finally ...

Some practical tips ...

1. Answer e-mails at the end of the day rather than the start. You will be amazed at how much more productive you feel by the end of the day.

2. Approach research leads and directors of research in schools, colleges and universities. Tell them who you are and what your research interests are – highlighting the research capacity-building potential you can contribute to.

3. If you are considering developing your research and writing profile, offer to review for practitioner and academic journals as part of a longer-term strategy targeting future publication.

4. If you are interested in presenting at conferences, offer to review abstracts for different conference organisations. This is a brilliant way to get to grips with the work and current thinking within your own research area.

5. If you work in a university, get to know the grant managers/university research funding officers so that if some opportunity comes up – even at the last minute – they immediately think of referring it to you!

6. If possible, widen your own methodological expertise in order to open more doors to future research collaborations.

7. If at all possible, seek out two mentors: one that works within your institution and one who works elsewhere. Both are likely to offer invaluable expertise while widening your own professional arena.

8. Seek out special interest groups and networks related to your own professional interests. Subject associations, university early career forums and academic networks can add invaluable professional capital to your own growing expertise.

9. With a colleague or two, put in a proposal for a special edition of a journal. It is fun and can raise your game in terms of developing professional expertise, networks and publishing craftsmanship.

10. Finally, if you have completed a doctorate, exploit its publishing potential to the maximum in terms of contributions to theory, practice, existing findings, methodology and policy.

IN A **NUTSHELL**

In the introduction chapter I mentioned that writing a book about teacher educators in the twenty-first century is teleologically problematic – not least when that writing has only occurred towards the end of the century's second decade. But I hope, nevertheless, that these chapters have offered an opportunity to critically reflect on the work we do as teacher educators, why we do it and in what ways we can strive to do it better. One of the many limitations of this book has been the fact that I have not been able to address, explicitly, issues related to the curriculum. And here I am immediately reminded of Cochran-Smith's (2016) '*equity turn*' (see Chapter 5), one predicated on the belief that many existing arrangements for teacher education do not currently ensure both excellence and equity for all students.

As we move at breathtaking speed through an intensely social, technological and cultural transformation, I do wonder to what extent our largely nineteenth-century curricular foundation is *fit-for-purpose* for teacher educators preparing teachers to teach young people who may be alive at the turn of the next century. We have written elsewhere (Czerniawski and Kidd, 2011) that all educational institutions need to recognise, understand and embrace twenty-first-century youth identities and reject outdated conceptions of childhood – conceptions that are redundant when dealing with the pervasiveness of cyber-bullying and online pornography. Young people, their teachers and their teachers' teachers need to feel trusted, valued and comfortable to change, experiment and take risks. Material conditions only partially (but significantly) determine and constrain initiatives in teacher education, as do the values and the existing commitments of teacher educators involved in those initiatives. This book has dedicated considerable time and energy to drawing attention to the variety of ways that teacher educators, as professional learners, can share best practices and develop their professionalism. The book celebrates the integrity, commitment and passion that teacher educators and teachers bring to their work and the improvements we make as we strive to improve our professional practice. But accompanying so many of these improvements, in the English context at least, is a pervasive form of instrumentalism – teacher education-by-numbers, if you like. This situation must change to one where teacher educators play a central role in re-thinking and re-defining current and future generations' conceptions of the importance and substance of both formal and informal education.

REFLECTIONS ON **CRITICAL ISSUES**

- *There is an understandable tendency for those of us working in teacher education to concentrate on our own immediate policy contexts and on our own institutional locations. However, as a profession we need to have a greater understanding of what it means to be a teacher educator in different national contexts, with a view to pivotally positioning this understanding at the heart of all teacher education courses. The look and feel of teaching, learning and research varies significantly from one national context to the next, as do the sorts of relationships that teacher educators and teachers cultivate with the variety of stakeholders they engage with. An understanding of these differences can help in critically reflecting on alternative conceptions of the nature and purpose of teacher education as part of a broader transformative approach to preparing teachers for the remainder of the twenty-first century.*

- *All research involves the identification of a research problem or question. It also involves identifying the procedures for capturing data and documenting analysis of this data while critically reflecting on these processes. This commitment to research is a powerful tool for encouraging professional autonomy and continuing reflective practice. It is also an opportunity to offer something of tremendous value to colleagues within and outside our own institutions. As such, it is an excellent means through which to continue our own professional development and professional learning.*

- *Thank you for reading this book and for doing the amazing work you do. I hope the ideas here help you in the future and I wish you every success in that endeavour.*

REFERENCES

Aberdeenshire Council (2017) Aberdeenshire Wins National Award. [online] Available at: https://online.aberdeenshire.gov.uk/apps/news/release.aspx?newsid=4816 (accessed 7 March 2018).

Association of Teacher Educators (ATE) (2017) Standards for Teacher Educators. [online] Available at: www.ate1.org/pubs/uploads/tchredstds0308.pdf (accessed 17 November 2017).

Akkerman, S and Bakker, A (2011) Boundary Crossing and Boundary Objects. *Review of Educational Research*, 81: 132–169.

Alexander, R J (2005) Education, Culture and Cognition: Intervening for Growth. International Association for Cognitive Education and Psychology (IACEP) 10th International Conference, University of Durham, UK, 10–14 July 2005.

Amott, P M (2016) Telling Stories: A Process of Identification for Six Neophyte Teacher Educators. PhD thesis (unpublished). London: UCL Institute of Education.

Apple, M (2005) Education, Markets and an Audit Culture. *Critical Quarterly*, 47(1–2): 11–29.

Bain, Y, Bruce, J and Weir, D (2016) Changing the Landscape of School/University Partnership in Northern Scotland. *Professional Development in Education*. DOI: 10.1080/19415257.2016.1231132.

Bain, Y, Dengerink, J and Gray, D (2017) Boundaries and Boundary Crossing. [online] Available at: http://info-ted.eu/boundaries/ (accessed 7 March 2018).

Ball, S (2012) The Making of a Neoliberal Academic. *Research in Secondary Education*, 2(1): 29–31.

Bates, T, Swennen, A and Jones, K (2011) *The Professional Development of Teacher Educators*. London: Routledge.

Bauman, Z (2004) *Wasted Lives: Modernity and Its Outcasts*. Cambridge: Polity Press.

Beauchamp, C and Thomas, L (2009) Understanding Teacher Identity: An Overview of Issues in the Literature and Implications for Teacher Education. *Cambridge Journal of Education*, 39(2): 175–199.

Beauchamp, G, Clarke, L, Hulme, M, Jephcote, M, Kennedy, A, Magennis, G, Menter, I, Murray, J, Mutton, T, O'Doherty, T and Peiser, G (2016) *Teacher Education in Times of Change*. Bristol: Policy Press.

Becher, T and Trowler, P (2002) *Academic Tribes and Territories: Intellectual Enquiry and the Culture of Disciplines*. Buckingham: SRHE and OUP.

Bennett, T (2016) *The School Research Lead*. London: The Education Development Trust.

Ben-Peretz, M, Kleeman, S, Reichenberg, R and Shimoni, S (2010) Educators of Educators: Their Goals, Perceptions and Practices. *Professional Development in Education*, 36(1–2): 111–129.

BERA-RSA (2014) Research and the Teaching Profession – Building the Capacity for a Self-improving Education System. Final Report of the BERA-RSA Inquiry into the Role of Research in Teacher Education. London: BERA.

Berry, A (2013) Teacher Educators' Professional Learning: A Necessary Case. Paper presented at the International Study Association of Teachers and Teaching (ISATT), Ghent, Belgium, 1–5 July.

Berry, A, Friedrichsen, P and Loughran, J (eds) (2015) *Re-examining Pedagogical Content Knowledge in Science Education* (pp 3–13). New York: Routledge.

Berry, B, Geursen, J and Lunenberg, M (2015) A Dialogue on Supporting Self-study Research in the Context of Dutch Teacher Education. In Samaras A and Pithouse-Morgan K (eds) *Polyvocal Professional Learning through Self-Study Research* (pp 39–56). Rotterdam, Boston, Taipei: Sense Publishers.

Billett, S (2010) Emerging Perspectives of Work: Implications for University Teaching and Learning. In Higgs, J, Fish, D, Golter, I, Loftus, S, Reid, J-A and Trede, F (eds) *Education for Future Practice* (pp 97–112). Rotterdam: Sense.

Boyd, P and Harris, K (2010) Becoming a University Lecturer in Teacher Education: Expert School Teachers Reconstructing Their Pedagogy and Identity. *Professional Development in Education*, 36(1–2): 9–24.

Boyd, P, Harris, K and Murray, J (2011) *Becoming a Teacher Educator: Guidelines for Induction*. Bristol: Higher Education Academy, Subject Centre for Education (ESCalate), University of Bristol Graduate School of Education.

Boyd, P and Szplit, A (eds) (2017) *Teachers and Teacher Educators Learning through Enquiry: International Perspectives*. Kraków: Wydawnictwo Attyka.

Boyd, P and Tibke, J (2012) Being a School-based Teacher Educator: Developing Pedagogy and Identity in Facilitating Work-based Higher Education in a Professional Field. *Practitioner Research in Higher Education*, 6(2): 41–57.

Braund, M (2015) Teacher Educators' Professional Journeys: Pedagogical and Systemic Issues Affecting Role Perceptions. *Africa Education Review*, 12(2): 309–330.

Britzman, D P (1992) The Terrible Problem of Knowing Thyself: Toward a Poststructural account of Teacher Identity. *JCT*, 9(3): 23–47.

Bullock, S M (2012) Creating a Space for the Development of Professional Knowledge: A Self-study of Supervising Teacher Candidates during Practicum Placements. *Studying Teacher Education*, 8: 143–156.

Busey, C L and Waters, S (2016) Who Are We? The Demographic and Professional Identity of Social Studies Teacher Educators. *The Journal of Social Studies Research*, 40: 71–83.

Carlson, J, Stokes, L, Helms, J, Gess-Newsome, J and Gardner, A (2015) The PCK Summit: A Process and Structure for Challenging Current Ideas, Providing Future Work and Considering New Directions. In Berry, A, Friedrichsen, P and Loughran, J (eds) *Re-examining Pedagogical Content Knowledge in Science Education* (pp 3–13). New York: Routledge.

Clarke, A (2001) The Recent Landscape of Teacher Education: Critical Points and Possible Conjectures. *Teaching and Teacher Education*, 17: 599–611.

Cochran-Smith, M (2003) Learning and Unlearning: The Education of Teacher Educators. *Teaching and Teacher Education*, 19: 5–28.

Cochran-Smith, M (2005) Teacher Educators as Researchers: Multiple Perspectives. *Teaching and Teacher Education*, 21: 219–225.

Cochran-Smith, M (2016) Foreword. In Beauchamp, G, Clarke, L, Hulme, M, Jephcote, M, Kennedy, A, Magennis, G, Menter, I, Murray, J, Mutton, T, O'Doherty, T and Peiser, G (eds) *Teacher Education in Times of Change*. Bristol: Policy Press.

Cochran-Smith, M, and Lytle, S L (1999) Relationships of Knowledge and Practice: Teacher Learning Communities. *Review of Research in Education*, 24: 249–305.

Cole, P (2004) *Professional Development: A Great Way to Avoid Change*. Seminar Series No 140, December 2004. Melbourne: IARTV.

Conway, P, Rust, F, Smith, K, Tack, H and Vanderlinde R (2015) InFo-TED: Bringing Policy, Research, and Practice Together around Teacher Educator Development. In Craig, C and Orland-Barak, L (eds) *International Teacher Education: Promising Pedagogies (Part C)*, Volume 22C (pp 341–364). Bingley: Emerald Insight.

Czerniawski, G (2010) *Emerging Teachers and Globalisation*. London: Routledge.

Czerniawski, G (2013) Professional Development for Professional Learners: Teachers' Experiences in Norway, Germany and England. *Journal of Education for Teaching* 39(4): 383–399.

Czerniawski, G, Gray, D, MacPhail, A, Bain, Y, Conway, P and Guberman, A (2018) The Professional Learning Needs and Priorities of Higher-Education Based Teacher Educators in England, Ireland and Scotland. *Journal of Education for Teaching*, 44(2): 133–148.

Czerniawski, G, Guberman, A and MacPhail, A (2017) The Professional Developmental Needs of Higher Education-based Teacher Educators: An International Comparative Needs Analysis. *European Journal of Teacher Education*, 40(1): 127–140.

Czerniawski, G and Kidd, W (2011) *The Student Voice Handbook – Bridging the Academic/Practitioner Divide*. London: Emerald.

Czerniawski, G, Kidd, W and Murray, J (2018) We Are All Teacher Educators Now: Understanding School-based Teacher Educators in Times of Change in England. In Swennen, A, Kosnic, C and Murray, J (eds) *International Research, Policy and Practice in Teacher Education: Insider Perspectives*. London: Springer.

Czerniawski, G and Ulvik, M (2014) Changing Contexts – Changing Landscapes. In Rabensteiner, P M (ed) *Internationalisation in Teacher Education* (pp 48–67). Baltmannsweiler: Schneider Verlag Hohengehren.

Darling-Hammond, L (2006) Constructing 21st Century Teacher Education. *Journal of Teacher Education*, 57(3): 300–314.

Darling-Hammond, L (2010) Teacher Education and the American Future. *Journal of Teacher Education*, 61(1): 35–47.

Darling-Hammond, L and Bransford, J (2005) *Preparing Teachers for a Changing World: What Teachers Should Learn and Be Able To Do*. San Francisco, CA: Jossey-Bass.

Darling-Hammond, L and Lieberman, A (2012) Teacher Education around the World: What Can We Learn from International Practice. In Darling-Hammond, L and Lieberman, A (eds) *Teacher Education around the World: Changing Policies and Practices* (pp 151–169). London: Routledge.

Davey, R (2013) *The Professional Identity of Teacher Educators. Career on the Cusp?* London: Routledge.

Davidson, I (2000) Without and Within: Inclusion, Identity and Continuing Education in New Wales. University of Wales, Bangor. Paper presented at SCUTREA 30th Annual Conference, 3–5 July.

Day, C and Sachs, J (2004) Professionalism, Performativity and Empowerment: Discourses in the Politics, Polices and Purposes of Continuing Professional Development. In Day, C and Sachs, J (eds) *International Handbook on the Continuing Professional Development of Teachers* (pp 3–32). Maidenhead: Open University Press.

Day, C and Sachs, J (2009) *International Handbook on the Continuing Professional Development of Teachers*. Maidenhead: Open University Press.

Day, C, Kington, A, Stobart, G and Sammons, P (2006) The Personal and Professional Selves of Teachers: Stable and Unstable Identities. *British Educational Research Journal*, 32(4): 601–616.

Dengerink, J (2016) Teacher Educators' Competencies: What Is Needed in a Multi-Faceted and Contested Profession. In Falus, I and Orgovanyi-Gajdos, J (eds) *New Aspects in European Teacher Education*. Eger: Liceum Kiado.

Dengerink, J, Lunenberg, M and Kools, Q (2015) What and How Teacher Educators Prefer to Learn. *Journal of Education for Teaching*, 41(1): 78–96. DOI: 10.1080/02607476.2014.992635.

Department for Education (2013) Teachers' Standards – Guidance for School Leaders, School Staff and Governing Bodies. July 2011 (introduction updated June 2013). [online] Available at: www.gov.uk/government/uploads/system/uploads/attachment_data/file/665520/Teachers__Standards.pdf (accessed 7 March 2018).

Dewey, J (1902) *The Child and the Curriculum*. Chicago, IL: University of Chicago Press.

Dinham, S (2012) Our Asian Schooling Infatuation: The Problem of PISA Envy, in *The Conversation*, published on 14 September 2012.

Donlevy, V, Meierkord, A and Rajania, A (2016) *Study on the Diversity within the Teaching Profession with Particular Focus on Migrant and/or Minority Background* – Final Report to DG Education and Culture of the European Commission. Brussels: European Commission.

Ducharme, E and Judge, H (1993) *The Lives of Teacher Educators: In Their Own Words*. New York: Teachers College Press.

Dymoke, S and Harrison, J K (2006) Professional Development and the Beginning Teacher: Issues of Teacher Autonomy and Institutional Conformity. *Journal of Education for Teaching*, 32(1): 71–92.

Earley, P and Bubb, S (2004) *Leading and Managing Continuing Professional Development: Developing Teachers, Developing Schools*. London: Sage/Paul Chapman.

Education Endowment Fund (EEF) (2017) Website extract downloaded 20 April 2017. [online] Available at: https://educationendowmentfoundation.org.uk/our-work/research-schools/ (accessed 7 March 2018).

Elliot, J (2007) Assessing the Quality of Action Research. *Research Papers in Education*, 22(2): 229–246.

Ellis, V, Glackin, G, Heighes, D, Norman, M, Nicol, S and Norris, K (2013) A Difficult Realization: The Proletarianisation of Higher Education-based Teacher Educators. *Journal of Education for Teaching: International Research and Pedagogy*, 39(3): 266–280.

Engeström, Y (2005) *Developmental Work Research: Expanding Activity Theory in Practice*. International Cultural-Historical Human Sciences Series Bd 12. Berlin: Lehmanns Media.

Eraut, M (2004) Informal Learning in the Workplace. *Studies in Continuing Education*, 26(2): 247–273.

Eraut, M and Hirsh, W (2007) *The Significance of Workplace Learning for Individuals, Groups and Organisations*. Skope Monograph 9. [online] Available at: www.skope.ox.ac.uk/wp-content/uploads/2014/12/Monogrpah-09.pdf (accessed 7 March 2018).

Eraut, M, Alderton, J, Cole, G and Senker, P (1998) Development of Knowledge and Skills in Employment. Final Report of a Research Project funded by 'The Learning Society' Programme of the Economic and Social Research Council: University of Sussex Institute of Education.

European Commission (2010) *Improving Teacher Quality: The EU Agenda – Lifelong Learning: Policies and Programme*. EAC.B.2. D (2010) PSH. Brussels: European Commission.

European Commission (2012) *Supporting the Teaching Professions for Better Learning Outcomes*. Commission Staff Working Document SWD (2012) 374. Strasbourg: European Commission.

European Commission (2013) *Supporting Teacher Educators for Better Learning Outcomes*. Brussels: European Commission. Report available at: http://ec.europa.eu/dgs/education_culture/repository/education/policy/school/doc/support-teacher-educators_en.pdf (accessed 7 March 2018).

European Commission (2015) *Strengthening Teaching in Europe: New Evidence from Teachers*. Compiled by Eurydice and CRELL, June 2015. Available at: http://ec.europa.eu/education/library/policy/teaching-profession-practices_en.pdf (accessed 7 March 2018).

Feiman-Nemser, S (2001) From Preparation to Practice: Designing a Continuum to Strengthen and Sustain Teaching. *Teachers College Record*, 103: 1013–1055.

Florian, L and Nataša Pantić, N (2013) *Learning to Teach: Part 1: Exploring the History and Role of Higher Education in Teacher Education*. London: Higher Education Academy.

Forgasz, R, Grimmett, H, White, S and Williams, J (2017) The Monash Casey Teaching Academy of Professional Practice Digital Resource. Available at: www.partnershipprojects.info/#about-the-monash-casey-tapp (accessed 21 January 2018).

Furlong, J and Lawn, M (eds) (2010) *Disciplines of Education: Their Role in the Future of Education Research*. London: Routledge.

Gaudelli, W and Ousley, D (2009) From Clothing to Skin: Identity Work of Student Teachers in Culminating Field Experiences. *Teaching and Teacher Education*, 25(6): 931–939.

Gewirtz, S (2013) Developing Teachers as Scholar-Citizens, Reasserting the Value of University Involvement in Teacher Education. In Florian, L and Pantić, N (eds) *Learning to Teach: Part 1: Exploring the History and Role of Higher Education in Teacher Education* (pp 10–13). London: Higher Education Academy.

Gewirtz, S, Mahony, P, Hextall, I and Cribb, A (2009) Policy, Professionalism and Practice: Understanding and Enhancing Teachers' Work. In Gewirtz, S, Mahony, P, Hextall, I, and Cribb, A (eds) *Changing Teacher Professionalism: International Trends, Challenges and the Way Forward* (pp 3–16). Oxon: Routledge.

Goffman, E (1959) *The Presentation of Self in Everyday Life*. Garden City, NJ: Doubleday.

Goodnough, K (2003) Facilitating Action Research in the Context of Science Education: Reflections of a University Researcher. *Educational Action Research*, 11(2): 41–64.

Goodwin, A L and Kosnik, C (2013) Quality Teacher Educators = Quality Teachers? Conceptualising Essential Domains of Knowledge for Those Who Teach Teachers. *Teacher Development*, 17(3): 334–346.

Goodwin, A L, Smith, L, Souto-Manning, M, Cheruvu, R, Tan, M Y, Reed, R and Taveras, L (2014) What Should Teacher Educators Know and Be Able to Do? Perspectives from Practicing Teacher Educators. *Journal of Teacher Education*, DOI:10.1177/0022487114535266.

Gordon, M and O'Brien, T V (eds) (2007) *Bridging Theory and Practice in Teacher Education*. Rotterdam: Sense.

Gove, M (2010) Speech to the National College for Leadership of Schools. 17 June 2010. [online] Available at: www.michaelgove.com/content/national_college_annual_conference (accessed 9 October 2017).

Gove, M (2014) I Refuse to Surrender to the Marxist Teachers Hell-bent on Destroying Our Schools: Education Secretary Berates 'the New Enemies of Promise' for Opposing His Plans. *Daily Mail*. [online] Available at: www.dailymail.co.uk/debate/article-2298146/I-refuse-surrender-Marxist-teachers-hell-bent-destroying-schools-Education-Secretary-berates-new-enemies-promise-opposing-plans.html (accessed 23 January 2018).

Gray, D (1999) Work-based Learning, Action Learning and the Virtual Paradigm, University of Surrey. Paper presented at the European Conference on Educational Research, Lahti, Finland, 22–25 September 1999.

Gray, D (2010) International Perspectives on Research in Initial Teacher Education and Some Emerging Issues. *Journal of Education for Teaching*, 36(4), 345–351. DOI: 10.1080/02607476.2010.513839.

Griffiths, V, Thompson, S and Hryniewicz, L (2014) Landmarks in the Professional and Academic Development of Mid-Career Teacher Educators. *European Journal of Teacher Education*, 37(1): 74–90.

Grimmet, P and Chinnery, A (2009) Bridging Policy and Professional Pedagogy in Teaching and Teacher Education: Buffering Learning by Education Teachers as Curriculum Makers. *Curriculum Inquiry*, 39(1): 125–143.

Groundwater-Smith, S and Mockler, N (2006) Research That Counts: Practitioner Research and the Academy. *Review of Australian Research in Education, 6. Special Edition of Australian Educational Researcher: Counterpoints on the Quality and Impact of Educational Research*, 105–117.

Hadar, L L and Brody, L D (2017) *Teacher Educators' Professional Learning*. New York: Routledge.

Hamilton, M L and Pinnegar, S (2015) *Knowing, Becoming, Doing as Teacher Educators: Identity, Intimate Scholarship, Inquiry*. Bingley: Emerald.

Hargreaves, A (2014) Foreword: Six Sources of Change in Professional Development. In Martin, L, Kragler, S, Quatroche, D J and Basuerman, K L (eds) *Handbook of Professional Development in Education* (pp x–xix). New York: The Guildford Press.

Hargreaves, A and Fullan, M (2012) Professional Capital – Transforming Teaching in Every School. New York: Teachers College Press.

Harrison, J and McKeon, F (2008) The Formal and Situated Learning of Beginning Teacher Educators in England: Identifying Characteristics for Successful Induction in the Transition from Workplace in Schools to Workplace in Higher Education. *European Journal of Teacher Education*, 31(2): 151–168.

Hartshorn, B, Hextall, I, Howell, I, Menter, I and Smyth, G (2005) Widening Access to the Teaching Profession. [online] Available at: www.gtcs.org.uk/web/FILES/FormUploads/widening-access-to-the-teaching-profession-full1765_326.pdf (last accessed 7 March 2018).

Hayhoe, R (2007) The Use of Ideal Types in Comparative Education: A Personal Reflection. *Comparative Education*, 43(2): 189–205.

Heggen, K (2008) Social Workers, Teachers and Nurses – from College to Professional Work. *Journal of Education and Work*, 21(3): 217–231.

Higgs, J (2011) Practice-based Education: Enhancing Practice and Pedagogy. Final Report for ALTC Teaching Fellowship. London: Australian Learning and Teaching Council.

Hodgkinson, H L (2002) Demographics and Teacher Education: An Overview. *Journal of Teacher Education*, 53(2): 102–105.

Hökkä, P (2012) Teacher Educators and Conflicting Demands – Tensions between Individual and Organizational Development. Academic (doctoral) dissertation published by University of Jyväskylä, Finland.

Hulme, M (2016) Analysing Teacher Education Policy: Comparative and Historical Approaches. In Beauchamp, G, Clarke L, Hulme M, Jephcote M, Kennedy A, Magennis G, Menter I, Murray J, Mutton T, O'Doherty T and Peiser G (eds) *Teacher Education in Times of Change* (pp 37–54). Bristol: Policy Press.

InFo-TED (2015) The Conceptual Model of Teacher Educators' Professionalism. Trondheim: Norwegian University of Science and Technology. [online] Available at: http://info-ted.eu/conceptual-model/ (accessed 7 March 2018).

Izadinia, M (2014) Teacher Educators' Identity: A Review of the Literature. *European Journal of Teacher Education*, 37(4): 426–441.

Jones, M, Stanley, G, McNamara, O and Murray, J (2011) Facilitating Teacher Educators' Professional Learning through a Regional Research Capacity-building Network. *Asia Pacific Journal of Teacher Education*, 39(3): 263–275.

Kant, I (1998) *Critique of Pure Reason*. Cambridge: Cambridge University Press.

Kelchtermans, G, Smith, K and Vanderlinde, R (2017) Towards an 'International Forum for Teacher Educator Development': An Agenda for Research and Action. *European Journal of Teacher Education*, DOI: 10.1080/02619768.2017.1372743

Kennedy, A (2005) Models of Continuing Professional Development: A Framework for Analysis. *Journal of In-service Education*, 31(2): 235–250.

Kidd, W (2012) Place, (Cyber) Space and Being: The Role of Student Voice in Informing the Un-situated Learning of Trainee Teachers. *Research in Secondary Teacher Education*, 2(1): 3–7.

Kidd, W (2016) Troubled Craft and Novice Teachers: An Ethnographic Account of Emerging Professional Identities of Novice Teachers in the English Lifelong Learning Sector. EdD thesis (unpublished). University of East London. [online] Available at: http://roar.uel.ac.uk/5892/1/Warren%20Kidd.pdf (accessed 7 March 2018).

Korthagen, F, Loughran, J and Russell, T (2006) Developing Fundamental Principles for Teacher Education Programmes and Practices. *Teaching and Teacher Education*, 22: 1020–1041.

Kosnik, C, Dharmashi, P, Miyata, C, Cleovoulou, Y and Beck, C (2015) Four Spheres of Knowledge Required: An International Study of the Professional Development of Literacy/English Teacher Educators. *Journal of Education for Teaching*, 4(1): 52–77.

Labaree, D F (2003) The Peculiar Problem of Preparing Educational Researchers. *Educational Researcher*, 32(4): 13–22.

Laudel, G and Glaser, J (2008) From Apprentice to Colleague: The Metamorphosis of Early Career Researchers. *Higher Education*, 55: 337–406.

Lave, J and Wenger, E (1991) *Situated Learning*. Cambridge: Cambridge University Press.

Leinhardt, G (1990) Capturing Craft Knowledge in Teaching. *Educational Researcher*, 19(2): 18–25.

Leonard, S N and Roberts, P (2016) No Time to Think: Policy, Pedagogy and Professional Learning. *Journal of Education Policy*, 31(2): 142–160. DOI: 10.1080/02680939.2015.1047801.

Lewin, K (1951) *Field Theory in Social Science: Selected Theoretical Papers*. New York: Harper & Brothers.

Lipowski, K, Jorde, D, Prenzel, M and Seidel, T (2011) Expert Views on the Implementation of Teacher Professional Development in European Countries. *Professional Development in Education*, 37(5): 685–700.

Livingston, K and Robertson, J (2001) The Coherent and the Empowered Individual: Continuing Professional Development for Teachers in Scotland. *European Journal of Education*, 24(2): 184–194.

Loucks-Horsley, S, Hewson, P W, Love, N B and Stiles, K E (1997) *Designing Professional Development for Teachers of Science and Mathematics*. Thousand Oaks, CA: Corwin.

Loughran, J (2006) *Developing a Pedagogy of Teacher Education*. London: Taylor & Francis.

Loughran, J (2014) Professionally Developing as a Teacher Educator. *Journal of Teacher Education*, 65(4): 1–13.

Lunenberg, M, Dengerink, J and Korthagen, F (2014) *The Professional Teacher Educators: Roles, Behaviour and Professional Development of Teachers*. Rotterdam: Sense Publications.

Lunenberg, M L, Korthagen, F and Zwart, R C (2010) Critical Issues in Supporting Self-study. *Teaching and Teacher Education,* 26(6): 1280–1289.

Lunenberg, M, Murray, J, Smith, K and Vanderlinde, R (2017) Collaborative Teacher Educator Development in Europe: Different Voices, One Goal. *Professional Development in Education*, 43(4): 556–572.

Lunenberg, M and Willemse, M (2006) Research and Professional Development of Teacher Educators. *European Journal of Teacher Education*, 19(1): 81–98. DOI:10.1080/02619760500478621.

Lyotard, J (1997) *Postmodern Fables*. Trans. Van Den Abbeele, G (ed). Minneapolis, MN: University of Minnesota Press, 1997. Translation of *Moralités postmodernes*. Paris: Galilée, 1993.

MacPhail, A, Patton, K, Parker, M and Tannehill, D (2014) Leading by Example: Teacher Educators' Professional Learning through Communities of Practice. *Quest*, 66: 39–56.

Maguire, M (2000) Inside/Outside the Ivory Tower: Teacher Education in the English Academy. *Teaching in Higher Education,* 5(2): 149–165.

Mannheim, K (1993) On the Interpretation of Weltanschauung. In Wolff, K H (ed) *From Karl Mannheim*. New Brunswick: Transaction Press.

Marshall, G (1998) *Dictionary of Sociology*. Oxford: Oxford University Press.

Marsick, V J (2009) Toward a Unifying Framework to Support Informal Learning Theory, Research and Practice. *Journal of Workplace Learning*, 21(4): 265–275.

Mattsson, M, Eilertson, T and Rorrison, D (eds) (2011) *A Practicum Turn in Teacher Education*. Rotterdam: Sense.

Mayer, D (2014) The Appropriation of the Professionalization Agenda in Teacher Education. *Research in Teacher Education*, 4(2): 39–44.

McAnulty, J and Cuenca, A (2014) Embracing Institutional Authority: The Emerging Identity of a Novice Teacher Educator. *Studying Teacher Education*, 10(1): 36–52.

McAleavy, T (2016) *Teaching as a Research-engaged Profession: Problems and Possibilities*. London: Education Development Trust.

McKeon, F and Harrison, J (2010) Developing Pedagogical Practice and Professional Identities of Beginning Teacher Educators. *Professional Development in Education,* 36(12): 25–44.

McMahon, M, Forde, C and Dickson, B (2015) Reshaping Teacher Education through the Professional Continuum. *Educational Review*, 67(2): 158–178.

McNamara, O and Murray, J (2013) The School Direct Programme and Its Implications for Research-informed Teacher Education and Teacher Educators. In Florian, L and Nataša Pantić, N (eds) *Learning to Teach: Part 1: Exploring the History and Role of Higher Education in Teacher Education*. London: Higher Education Academy.

McNamara, O, Murray, J and Jones, M (2014) *Workplace Learning in Teacher Education*. Singapore: Springer.

McNamara, O, Murray, J and Phillips, R (2017) *Policy and Research Evidence in the 'Reform' of Primary Initial Teacher Education in England*. York: Cambridge Primary Review Trust.

Menter, I (2015) From the President. *Research Intelligence*, 127: 4–5. London: British Educational Research Association.

Murray, J (2002) Between the Chalkface and the Ivory Towers? A Study of the Professionalism of Teacher Educators Working on Primary Initial Teacher Education Courses in the English Education System. *Collected Original Resources in Education (CORE)*, 26(3): 1–530.

Murray, J (2011) Towards a New Language of Scholarship in Teacher Educators' Professional Learning. In Bates, T, Swennen, A and Jones, K (eds) *The Professional Development of Teacher Educators*. London: Routledge.

Murray, J (2014) Teacher Educators' Constructions of Professionalism: A Case Study. *Asia-Pacific Journal of Teacher Education*, 42(1): 7–21.

Murray, J, Czerniawski, G and Barber, P (2014) Teacher Educators' Identities and Work in England at the Beginning of the Second Decade of the Twenty-first Century. In Murray, J and Kosnik, C (eds) *Academic Work and Identities in Teacher Education* (pp 21–39). London: Routledge.

Murray, J, Czerniawski, G and Kidd, W (2013) Understanding Teacher Educators' Work and Knowledge: Multiple Perspectives. Paper presented at the BERA Annual Conference, University of Sussex, United Kingdom. 4 September 2013.

Murray, J, Lunenberg, M and Smith, K (2017) Educating the Educators: Policies and Initiatives in European Teacher Education. In Peters, M A, Cowie, B and Mentor, I (eds) *A Companion to Research in Teacher Education* (pp 651–666). Singapore: Springer Nature.

Murray, J and Male, T (2005) Becoming a Teacher Educator: Evidence from the Field. *Teaching and Teacher Education*, 21(2): 125–142.

Murray, J and Mutton, T (2016) Teacher Education in England: Change in Abundance, Continuities in Question. In Beauchamp, G, Clarke, L, Hulme, M, Jephcote, M, Kennedy, A, Magennis, G, Menter, I, Murray, J, Mutton, T, O'Doherty, T and Peiser, G (eds) *Teacher Education in Times of Change* (pp 57–74). Bristol: Policy Press.

Mutton, T, Burn, K and Menter, I (2017) Deconstructing the Carter Review: Competing Conceptions of Quality in England's 'School-led' System of Initial Teacher Education. *Journal of Education Policy*, 32(1): 14–33.

NCTL (National College for Teaching and Leadership) (2014) Teaching Schools: National Research and Development Network. [online] Available at: www.gov.uk/collections/teaching-schools-national-research-and-development (accessed 7 March 2018).

Newbury, M (2014) Teacher Educator Identity Development of the Nontraditional Teacher Educator. *Studying Teacher Education*, 10(2): 163–178.

Noddings, N (1992) The Challenge to Care in Schools: An Alternative Approach to Education. *Advances in Contemporary Educational Thought,* vol 8. New York: Teachers College Press.

O'Dwyer, J B and Atli, H H (2015) A Study of In-service Teacher Educator Roles, with Implications for a Curriculum for Their Professional Development. *European Journal of Teacher Education,* 38(1): 4–20.

OECD (2005) *Teachers Matter: Attracting, Developing and Retaining Effective Teachers.* Paris: OECD Publications.

OECD (2010) *The High Cost of Low Educational Performance.* Paris: OECD Publications.

OECD (2015) *Frascati Manual 2015: Guidelines for Collecting and Reporting Data on Research and Experimental Development.* Paris: OECD Publications.

OECD (2017) *Education at a Glance (2017).* Paris: OECD Publications.

Ozga, J and Jones, R (2006) Travelling and Embedded Policy: The Case of Knowledge Transfer. *Journal of Education Policy*, 21(1): 1–17.

Payne, K A and Zeichner, K (2017) Multiple Voices and Participants in Teacher Education. In Clandinin, J D and Husu, J (eds) *The Sage Handbook of Research on Teacher Education* (pp 1101–1116). London: Sage.

Peiser, G (2016) The Place of Research in Teacher Education. In Beauchamp, G, Clarke, L, Hulme, M, Jephcote, M, Kennedy, A, Magennis, G, Menter, I, Murray, J, Mutton, T, O'Doherty, T and Peiser, G (eds) *Teacher Education in Times of Change* (pp 161–178). Policy Press: Bristol.

Philpott, C (2014) *Theories of Professional Learning – A Critical Guide for Teacher Educators.* Northwich: Critical Publishing.

Putnam, R and Borko, H (2000) What Do New Views of Knowledge and Thinking Have to Say about Research on Teacher Learning? *Educational Researcher*, 29(1): 4–15.

Research Excellence Framework (2014) The Results. [online] Available at: www.ref.ac.uk/2014/media/ref/content/pub/REF%2001%202014%20-%20full%20document.pdf (accessed 7 March 2018).

Research Excellence Framework (2015) Overview Report by Main Panel C and Sub-panels 16–26, p 101. [online] Available at: www.ref.ac.uk/2014/media/ref/content/expanel/member/Main%20Panel%20C%20over-view%20report.pdf (accessed 7 March 2018).

Roberts, N (2000) Wicked Problems and Network Approaches to Resolution. *International Public Management Review*, 1(1): 1–19.

Russell, T (1997) Teaching Teachers: How I Teach IS the Message. In Loughran, J and Russell, T (eds) *Teaching about Teaching: Purpose, Passion and Pedagogy in Teacher Education* (pp 32–47). London: Falmer Press.

Sahlberg, P (2012) Global Educational Reform Movement Is Here. [online] Available at: https://pasisahlberg.com/global-educational-reform-movement-is-here/ (accessed 24 January 2018).

Santorro, N (2009) Teaching in Culturally Diverse Contexts: What Knowledge about 'Self' and 'Others' Do Teachers Need? *Journal of Education for Teaching*, 35(1): 33–45.

Schön, D A (1983) *The Reflective Practitioner: How Professionals Think in Action*. New York: Basic Books.

Sennett, R (2008) *The Craftsman*. London: Penguin Books.

Shulman, L (1987) Knowledge and Teaching: Foundations of the New Reform. *Harvard Educational Review*, 57(1): 1–23.

Shulman, L (2015) PCK: Its Genesis and Exodus. In Berry, A, Friedrichsen, P and Loughran, J (eds) *Re-examining Pedagogical Content Knowledge in Science Education* (pp 3–13). New York: Routledge.

Smith, K (2003) So What About the Professional Development of Teacher Educators? *European Journal of Teacher Education*, 26(2): 201–215.

Smith, K (2015) The Role of Research in Teacher Education. *Research in Teacher Education*, 5(2): 43–46.

Smith, K (2016) Functions of Assessment in Teacher Education. In Hamilton, M L and Loughran, J J (eds) *The International Handbook of Teacher Education* (pp 405–428). Dordrecht: Springer.

Stern, N (2016) *Building on Success and Learning from Experience: An Independent Review of the Research Excellence Framework*. London: Department of Business, Energy and Industrial Strategy. [online] Available at: www.gov.uk/government/uploads/system/uploads/attachment_data/file/541338/ind-16-9-ref-stern-review.pdf (accessed 29 March 2018).

Stoll, L and Earl, L (2011) *Realising the Power of Professional Learning*. Maidenhead: Open University Press.

Suchman, L (1994) Working Relations of Technology Production and Use. *Computer Supported Cooperative Work*, 2(21): 21–39.

Swennen, A (2014) More than Just a Teacher: The Identity of Teacher Educators. In Jones, K and White, E (eds) *Developing Outstanding Practice in School-based Teacher Education*. Northwich: Critical Publishing.

Swennen, A, Jones, K and Volman, M (2010) Teacher Educators: Their Identities, Sub-Identities and Implications for Professional Development. *Professional Development in Education*, 36(1–2): 131–148.

Tack, H and Vanderlinde, R (2014) Teacher Educators' Professional Development: Towards a Typology of Teacher Educators' Researcherly Disposition. *British Journal of Educational Studies*, 62(3): 297–315.

Tack, H and Vanderlinde, R (2016) Measuring Teacher Educators' Researcherly Disposition: Item Development and Scale Construction. *Vocations and Learning*. DOI: 10.1007/s12186-016-9148-5.

Tatto, M T, Schwille, J, Senk, S, Ingvarson, L, Peck, R and Rowley, G (2008) *Teacher Education and Development Study in Mathematics (TEDS-M): Policy, Practice, and Readiness to Teach Primary and Secondary Mathematics. Conceptual Framework*. East Lansing, MI: Teacher Education and Development International Study Center, College of Education, Michigan State University.

Teacher Education Group (2016) *Teacher Education in Times of Change*. Bristol: Policy Press.

Tryggvason, M (2012) Perceptions of Identity among Finnish University-based Subject Teacher Educators. *European Journal of Teacher Education*, 35(3): 289–303.

Ulriksen, L (1995) General Qualification and Teacher Qualification in the Vocational Training System. PhD dissertation (unpublished). Adult Education Research Group, Roskilde University.

Van der Klink, M, Kools, Q, Avissar, G, White, S and Sakata, T (2017) Professional Development of Teacher Educators: What Do They Do? Findings from an Explorative International Study. *Professional Development in Education*, 43(2): 163–178.

Van Driel, J H and Berry, A K (2017) Developing Pre-service Teachers' Pedagogical Content Knowledge. In Clandinin, J D and Husu, J (eds) *The Sage Handbook of Research on Teacher Education*. London: Sage.

van Helzen, C, van der Klink, M, Swennen, A and Yaffe, E (2011) The Induction and Needs of Beginning Teacher Educators. In Bates, T, Swennen, A and Jones, K (eds) *The Professional Development of Teacher Educators* (pp 61–75). London: Routledge.

van Helzen, C and Volman, M (2009) The Activities of a School-based Teacher Educator: A Theoretical and Empirical Exploration. *European Journal of Teacher Education*, 32(4): 345–367.

Vanassche, E and Kelchtermans, G (2015) The State of the Art in Self-study of Teacher Education Practices: A Systematic Review. *Journal of Curriculum Studies*. DOI:10.1080/ 00220272.2014.995712.

Vanassche, E, Rust, F, Conway, P, Smith, K, Tack, H and Vanderlinde, R (2015) InFo-TED: Bringing Policy, Research, and Practice Together Around Teacher Educator Development. In Craig, C and Orland-Barak, L (eds) *International Teacher Education: Promising Pedagogies* (pp 341–364). Bingley: Emerald Publishing.

Victoria State Government (2017) *Teaching Academies of Professional Practice*. Victoria State Government website. [online] Available at: www.education.vic.gov.au/about/programs/partnerships/Pages/tapp.aspx (accessed 21 January 2018)

Wenger, E (1998) *Communities of Practice: Learning, Meaning and Identity*. Cambridge: Cambridge University Press.

Wenger, E (2009) A Social Theory of Learning. In Illeris, K (ed) *Contemporary Theories of Learning. Learning Theorists … in Their Own Words* (pp 209–218). New York: Routledge.

Westrup, R and Jackson, A (2009) The Professional Development Needs of Teacher Educators in Higher Education Institutions (HEIs) and School-based Mentors in Schools. ESCalate Initial Teacher Education (ITE) at the University of Cumbria. [online] Available at: www.heacademy.ac.uk/knowledge-hub/professional-development-needs-teacher-educators-higher-education-institutions-heis (accessed 7 March 2018).

White, E (2013) Exploring the Professional Development Needs of New Teacher Educators Situated Solely in School: Pedagogical Knowledge and Professional Identity. *Professional Development in Education*, 39(1): 82–98.

White, E (2017) Developing Research-rich Teaching Practices as an Experienced Teacher Educator. Paper presented at the European Educational Research Association (ECER) Annual Conference, 25 August 2017. University College (UCC) Copenhagen, Denmark.

White, E, Dickerson, C and Weston, K (2015) Developing an Appreciation of What It Means to be a School-based Teacher Educator. *European Journal of Teacher Education*, 38(4): 445–459.

Whiting, C, Whitty, G, Menter, I, Black, P, Hordern, J, Parfitt, A, Reynolds, K and Sorenson, N (2018) Diversity and Complexity: Becoming a Teacher in England in 2015–16. *Review of Education*, in press.

Whitty, G with Anders, J, Hayton, A, Tang, S and Wisby, E (2016) *Research in Policy and Education*. London: UCL IoE Press.

Wilkins, C and Wood, P (2009) Initial Teacher Education in the Panopticon. *Journal of Education for Teaching*, 35(3): 283–297.

Willemse, T M and Boei, F (2017) Supporting Teacher Educators' Professional Development in Research and Supervising Students' Research. In Boyd, P and Szplit, A (eds) *Teachers and Teacher Educators Learning Through Enquiry: International Perspectives* (pp 197–216). Krakow: Wydawnictwo Attyka.

Williams, J (2013) Boundary Crossing and Working in the Third Space: Implications for a Teacher Educator's Identity and Practice. *Studying Teacher Education*, 9(2): 118–129.

Williams, J and Ritter, J (2010) Constructing New Professional Identities through Self-study: From Teacher to Teacher Educator. *Professional Development in Education*, 36(1): 77–92.

Williams, J, Ritter, J and Bullock, S M (2012) Understanding the Complexity of Becoming a Teacher Educator: Experience, Belonging and Practice within a Professional Learning Community. *Studying Teacher Education*, 8(3): 245–260.

Zeichner, K (1999) The New Scholarship in Teacher Education. *Educational Researcher*, 28(9): 4–15. DOI: 10.3102/0013189X028009004.

Zeichner, K (2010) Rethinking the Connections between Campus Courses and Field Experiences in College- and University-based Teacher Education. *Journal of Teacher Education*, 61(1–2): 89–99.

INDEX